Edward Armstrong

The French Wars of Religion

their political aspects - an expansion of three lectures delivered before the

Oxford University Extension summer meeting of August 1892

Edward Armstrong

The French Wars of Religion
their political aspects - an expansion of three lectures delivered before the Oxford University Extension summer meeting of August 1892

ISBN/EAN: 9783337816063

Printed in Europe, USA, Canada, Australia, Japan

Cover: Foto ©Suzi / pixelio.de

More available books at **www.hansebooks.com**

THE
FRENCH WARS OF RELIGION

Their Political Aspects

AN EXPANSION OF THREE LECTURES
DELIVERED BEFORE THE OXFORD UNIVERSITY EXTENSION
SUMMER MEETING OF AUGUST, 1892

BY

E. ARMSTRONG, M.A.

FELLOW OF QUEEN'S COLLEGE

London
PERCIVAL & CO.
1892

CONTENTS

	PAGE
GENEALOGY SHOWING CONNECTION OF THE HOUSES OF VALOIS AND BOURBON	v
GENEALOGY SHOWING CONNECTION OF THE HOUSES OF MONTMORENCI, CHÂTILLON, AND CONDÉ . . .	vi
GENEALOGY OF THE HOUSES OF LORRAINE AND GUISE .	vii
CHRONOLOGICAL SUMMARY	ix
I. THE HUGUENOTS	1
II. THE LEAGUE	45
III. THE CROWN	84
INDEX . . .	125

CHRONOLOGICAL SUMMARY

FIRST PERIOD.

1559. Treaty of Cateau Cambrésis between France and Spain (April). Death of Henry II. at a Tournament. Accession of Francis II. Supremacy of the Guises, uncles of the Queen.

1560. La Renaudie's Conspiracy, the Tumult of Amboise (March). Edict of Romorantin against the Huguenots. Arrest and sentence of Condé. Death of Francis II (Dec.). Accession of Charles IX. under guardianship of Catherine di Medici and Anthony of Navarre.

1561. Estates General of Orleans (Jan.). The Catholic triumvirate—Guise, Montmorenci, S. André. Estates of Pontoise (Aug.). Colloquy of Poissi between Catholic and Calvinist divines (Sept.).

1562. The tolerant Edict of January. Navarre joins the Catholics. Massacre of the Congregation of Vassi by Guise's followers (March). Condé and Coligni seize Orleans (April). English at Havre. Capture of Rouen by Catholics (Oct.), and death of Navarre. Defeat of Huguenots at Dreux. Capture of Condé and Montmorenci. Death of S. André.

1563. Murder of Guise before Orleans by Poltrot (Feb.). Peace of Amboise (March). Capture of Havre from English (July).

1564. Peace of Troyes with English. Tour of Catherine and Charles.

1565. Their interview with Elizabeth of Spain and Alva at Bayonne (June).

1566. Troubles in the Netherlands.

1567. Second War. Attempt of Condé to seize the Court at Meaux (Sept.). Condé attacks Paris. Battle of S. Denis. Death of Montmorenci (Nov.).

1568. John Casimir's Germans join Condé. Peace of Longjumeau or Chartres (March). Flight of Condé and Coligni (Aug.). Third War. Orange driven into France.

1569. Defeat of Huguenots at Jarnac (March). Death of Condé. Invasion of Deux Ponts. Defeat of Coligni at Moncontour (Oct.). Defence of S. Jean d'Angely. Louis of Nassau at Rochelle.

1570. Peace of S. Germain (Aug.).

1571-2. French schemes on Netherlands. Anglo-French alliance. Louis of Nassau with French aid seizes Valenciennes and Mons. Marriage of Navarre and Margaret. Massacre of S. Bartholomew (Aug.).

SECOND PERIOD.

1572. Navarre and Condé abjure Reform. Local resistance of Huguenot towns. The Fourth War.

1573. Sieges of Rochelle and Sancerre. Negotiations of the Crown with Orange. The Fair of Frankfort. Election of Anjou to throne of Poland (May). Peace of Rochelle (June).

1574. Fifth War. Conspiracy of Navarre and Alençon—its discovery. Execution of La Mole and Coconas. Arrest of Marshals Montmorenci and Cossé. Death of Charles IX. (May). Negotiations for marriage of Alençon with Elizabeth (1573-4). Confederation of Huguenots and Politiques under Damville in Languedoc. Return of Henry III. from Poland (Sept.). Death of Cardinal of Lorraine (Dec.).

1575. Escape and revolt of Alençon. Invasion of John Casimir (Sept.).

1576. Escape of Navarre (Feb.). Alençon, John Casimir, and Condé march on Paris. Peace of Monsieur (April). Its favourable terms for the Huguenots. Catholic League of Picardy (June). Estates General of Blois and Catholic revival.

1577. The Sixth War (March). Peace of Bergerac (Sept.).

1578. Alençon in the Netherlands. Growing antagonism to the Crown.

1579. Alençon in England. French occupation of Cambrai and La Fère.

1580. Seventh or Lovers' War (Feb.). Peace of Fleix (Nov.). Treaty of Plessis between Alençon and United Provinces. Henry recognises Alençon's expedition to Netherlands. France to annex Artois.

1581. Alençon lord of the Netherlands; his visit to England and betrothal to Elizabeth.

1582. Alençon in the Netherlands. Catherine interferes for independence of Portugal. Defeat of French fleet off Azores.

1583. Alençon's treacherous attempt on Antwerp (Jan.).

1584. Alençon's death (June). Assassination of Orange (July).

THIRD PERIOD.

1584. The League of Paris (Dec.).
1585. The Pact of Joinville between Guises, Cardinal Bourbon, and Spanish agents (Jan.). Henry III. refuses the sovereignty of the Netherlands (Feb.).
1587. War of the 'Three Henries.' Navarre defeats Joyeuse at Coutras (Oct.). The King makes terms with the German auxiliaries who are cut to pieces by Guise (Nov.). Remarkable retreat of the Huguenot horse.
1588. The day of the Barricades (May). The King forced to fly from Paris. His capitulation to the League. The Estates General of Blois. Murder of Henry of Guise and the Cardinal of Guise by the King (Dec.).
1589. Death of Catherine di Medici (Jan.). The Revolution at Paris. League of the King and Navarre. Their march on Paris. Murder of Henry III. by Clément (Aug.).

FOURTH PERIOD.

1589. Two Bourbon Kings, Henry IV. and Charles X. Henry's retreat from Paris to Normandy. His victory over Mayenne at Arques. Differences between Mayenne and the Sixteen at Paris. Spanish influence in Paris.
1590. Henry's victory at Ivry (March). Siege and starvation of Paris. Death of Charles X. (May). The Duke of Parma relieves the town (Sept.).
1591. The Royalists capture S. Denis, blockade Paris, and take Chartres. Terrorism of the Sixteen and their suppression by Mayenne.
1592. Siege of Rouen and its relief by Parma. His retreat to the Netherlands and death (Dec.).
1593. Estates of the League. Who is to be the Catholic King? Struggle against Spanish influence. Henry IV.'s abjuration of heresy (July).
1594. Henry IV. enters Paris (March). Gradual extinction of the League.
1595. War declared against Spain (Jan.). The King's absolution by Clement VIII. (Sept.).
1596. Submission of Mayenne. The Spaniards surprise Calais (April).
1597. The Spaniards surprise Amiens (March). Its re-capture (Sept.).
1598. Brittany conquered from Mercœur. The last of the League. Edict of Nantes (April). Peace of Vervins with Spain (May).

ERRATA.

Page 15, line 9, for "subjecting" read "submitting."
,, 16 ,, 33, ,, "it" read "Reform."
,, 22 ,, 24, ,, "separations" read "separatism."
,, 26 ,, 22, ,, "them" read "them not."
,, 30 ,, 17, ,, "nobilty" read "nobility."
,, 52 ,, 30, ,, ", or to," read "it to."

I.

THE HUGUENOTS

EVERY great religious or spiritual movement is likely, sooner or later, to take a political direction. It will associate with itself the aspirations and the grievances of classes which are on the rise or which are oppressed; it will serve sometimes as a help, more often as a hindrance to the actual government. The movement will frequently begin by combating and counteracting pre-existent political tendencies, but will as a rule in the end accentuate and stimulate them, hastening the decline of the falling and the ascent of the rising, providing a programme and a war cry, bringing forces, long sullenly adverse, to the fighting point.

If this principle is true of any religious movement, it is certainly true of the Reformation, which left its political traces on every country in Europe where it obtained a footing. These are not to be ascribed to the characteristics of this religion or of that, but to the mere fact of a great religious struggle which brought all disputed questions to an issue. It was antecedently probable that the Reformation would be absorbed by a people so peculiarly receptive as the French, and it had great political opportunities in the *malaise* resulting from more than half a century of foreign wars, and in the discontent with the absolutism of a monarchy at once omnipotent and incompetent. It is of interest, therefore, to trace the effects of the Wars of Religion upon the political system of France, to estimate their influence upon the elements which formed the State, upon the Crown, the Church, the nobility, the towns, the people, upon the great constitutional institutions, the Estates General, and the Law Courts or so-called Parliaments; upon political theory, that is, upon the opinions held as to the relations of Crown to People.

The development of Huguenotism as a form of religious belief is beyond our purpose. Nor is it possible to dwell upon the persecutions of Francis I., though it may be remembered that in suppressing religious heterodoxy, the King believed that he was stamping out social and political disaffection, into which the more orthodox cruelty of his son Henry II. rapidly transformed it. Some points, however, in the early formative religious period require consideration, especially the affiliation to the Genevan system, and the class distribution of Reform. The dissentients were long called Lutherans, but had French Reform been Lutheran it could hardly have culminated in revolt against the State. Since the Religious Peace of Augsburg, Lutheranism was so entirely part and parcel of the State system, that a split was well-nigh impossible. In France, Lutheranism could only have been practicable if the Crown had placed itself at the head of the Reforming movement; if it had enlarged its conception of Gallican liberties so far as to embrace dogma; if it had translated in a Protestant sense its maxim, *Une foi, une loi, un Roi*, which was after all the counterpart of the Lutheran principle, *Cujus regio, ejus religio*.

It was of importance also that French Reform was too late to be seriously affected by the Socialistic theories of Anabaptism, which in their extreme form had been crushed out at Münster. Anabaptism indeed of an indigenous and indeterminate character was seething in the great commercial centres of the Netherlands, but even here it was being at once modified and organized by the importation of Calvinist teaching. This left wing of Reform was, moreover, geographically, socially, and ethnologically separated from the French districts upon which the new doctrines gained hold. Artois and Hainault, which were mainly Catholic, rural, and aristocratic, separated the Flemish sectaries from Picardy and Champagne, which also were among the less impressionable and less commercial of French provinces. The unemployed proletariate of Ghent and Antwerp, starving from bad financial administration and English competition, had little in common with the prosperous bourgeoisie of France, or even with the handicraftsmen of the riverain towns. If we except Arras, Valenciennes, and Lille, the early sectaries of the Netherlands were of Flemish origin, and looked rather to Germany or England than to France. Thus French Reform grew up unfettered by the trammels of Erastianism, and untinged except in isolated instances by the socialistic theories of the Anabaptists. The latter indeed attempted to utilize the early disturbances, but were suppressed with the full sympathy of the Reformers themselves.

For purposes of resistance, the Genevan system had peculiar advantages. The congregations, the consistories, the synods—could, as they stood, be easily converted into political sections; they could readily form the *cadres* of a military organization; they were peculiarly adapted to tap or to drain the financial resources of the party. The material strength of Calvinism is proved by the resistance offered in France to an overwhelming Catholic majority, backed by the resources of the Crown, whereas in Bavaria and Austria a nobility and people almost entirely Lutheran succumbed to governments possessed of small resources.

The Reformation in France seems first to have affected mainly the lower classes, and the religious orders, precisely as was the case in Germany. We possess the official registers of the sentences passed by the Chambre Ardente of Henry II,* which generally give the profession of those convicted.

* *La Chambre Ardente*, by N. Weiss, Paris, 1889. For a notice of this book see *English Hist. Rev.*, vol. v.

They are drawn chiefly from the small tradesman, or artisan class, from domestic servants, or petty officials. Several of the religious orders were deeply infected, more especially the Franciscans; it was found necessary to subject many monasteries to a rigorous visitation. On the other hand, the parochial clergy were stoutly orthodox, one of the few exceptions being the incumbent of Bray, who, unlike the English vicar of his name, suffered for his faith. It is possible that persecution was successful among these classes, for when the war had broken out, dissent was not as a rule found among the populace, while the monks and friars proved the *corps d'élite* of Catholicism. It must be remembered, moreover, that, in the winter of 1548-9, many of the gentry and men of means were able to take refuge at Geneva; among them the handsome and aristocratic prior Déode de Bèze. Moreover, both civil and ecclesiastical officials seem to have shrunk from attacking men of recognized position.*

The methods by which the Crown attempted to enforce persecution had an immediate political effect. The Government largely increased the powers of the Ecclesiastical Courts, and, *pari passu*, detracted from those of the regular Law Courts called the Parliaments. The Parliament of Paris protested not only against the infringement of its privileges, but against conversion by persecution, and the same feelings existed at Rouen, where several members had to be excluded for heretical opinions. The introduction of the Spanish form of inquisition, under a Bull of Paul IV., in 1557, still further exasperated the profession. The Inquisitors were directed to appoint diocesan tribunals, which should decide without appeal. The Parliament of Paris flatly refused to register the

* The registers of the Chambre Ardente only concern the *ressort* of the Parliament of Paris. It is probable that in the south, and perhaps in Normandy, Reform was from the first more common among the wealthier classes. Cognac was nearly the southernmost town of the *ressort* of Paris, and the victims from here were merchants.

royal edict, and continued to receive appeals. The finale was the celebrated Wednesday meeting of the assembled chambers, the Mercuriale, where the King in person interfered with the constitutional freedom of speech, and ordered the arrest of the five members, thus giving his verdict for the ultra Catholic minority of Parliament against the moderate majority. Marshal Vielleville, himself a sound Catholic, strongly dissuaded this course of action. Its result was that one of the most influential elements of the State was not indeed brought into connection with Reform, but was placed in an attitude of hostility to the Government, and as the grievance was the consequence of the religious policy of the Crown, it had at all events a tendency to bring about a *rapprochement* between the Reformers and the judicial classes.

The growth of Reform was, however, more directly affected by the foreign wars. They made it difficult for the executive to deal efficiently with the evil; the local authorities were often indisposed to act up to their orders. Moreover, though the French troops were carefully kept from direct contact with their Lutheran allies, yet the fact that the national enemy was the great Catholic power must have had its weight.*

If the war favoured the growth of Reform, the Peace of Cateau Cambrésis brought the movement to a head. From a territorial point of view it was not so disadvantageous to France as was thought at the time. But its significance was that it was the † close of the national wars which had begun with Charles VIII., and the beginning of the religious wars, which were not to be completely laid but by the spell of Richelieu. The celebrated tale of William of Orange, con-

---

* Dissent had early outgrown the possibilities of persecution. Whole towns, wrote a Tuscan ambassador in 1546, lived completely in Protestant fashion, not, of course, openly, but in private by tacit consent, and among them were Caen, Rochelle, and Poitiers. In 1558 the Venetian Soranzo wrote that the Lutherans numbered 40,000, with such a perfect system of organization and communication that it would be extremely hard to find any means of checking the evil.

cerning the definite understanding between the two kings for mutual aid in suppressing heresy, is probably apocryphal. It appears first long after the event in William's *Apologia*, and is contradicted by strong contemporary evidence. Yet both kings unquestionably had heresy in view, and the military classes, who considered the peace in itself dishonourable, disliked the object of the peace. But its effect was even more direct than this. The great men who had Court offices or Crown benefices suffered little, but the military class was ruined by peace. The smaller nobility* found their estates crippled by war, they had long lived upon pay or plunder, the younger sons had no profession but arms, for even ecclesiastical benefices were more and more confined to the Court circle. They in vain applied to the Government for employment. Hence universal discontent with the administration, especially with the Cardinal of Lorraine its chief, the most formidable enemy of Reform.

Meanwhile the Reformers had become more powerful, and were in more immediate peril. The reign of Henry II. had been the period of organization. In 1555 churches had been established in many towns of Central and Southern France on the Geneva model.

Coincident with the Mercuriale of 1559 was the organization of the union of the churches, with full machinery of local consistories, provincial synods, and a national meeting, all on the elective system, and all containing a lay and a clerical element in equal proportions. This organization in the face of danger became political, and even military. The smaller nobles went over in large numbers to Reform, and transformed

---

* English readers are apt to be misled by the phrase "nobility." Among the French nobility the eldest son received the bulk of the family estates. The lesser country nobles in wealth or mode of life hardly differed from the small farmers among whom they lived, and with whom they associated on easy terms. All that separated them from their neighbours was "privilege," and to this they clung the more desperately.

its character. From being a long-suffering and patient sect, it became political, aggressive, at times oppressive.

It was of service to the Huguenots that the Peace of Cateau Cambrésis was immediately followed by the fatal tournament which cost Henry II. his life. Politically a puppet, he was physically a man, and a fine man. His successor was a boy, and a feeble boy, under the influence of his wife Mary Stuart, who was under the influence of her uncles, the Guises. Discontent found its voice because the demoralisation of the Monarchy, if not more real, was more obvious.

Personal monarchy, if weak, becomes a prey to personal faction. The favour of Henry and his mistress Diana had been divided between two families, the House of Montmorenci, and the House of Guise. The former belonged to the highest rank of non-royal French nobility, and its head, the Duke, possessed the highest official rank as Constable. He had capable sons, and equally capable nephews, his sister's three sons, the Châtillons. Of these, Gaspard Coligni was Admiral of France, D'Andelot commanded the infantry within the limits of France, while Odet obtained a Cardinal's hat. With them were associated members of the Royal House of Bourbon, the sons of the Duke of Vendôme. Antony, the eldest, was first Prince of the Blood, and by his marriage with Jeanne d'Albret won the title of King of Navarre. Condé, the youngest, had married the Constable's great-niece, Eleanor of Roye. On the defection of the Constable Bourbon, the line of Vendôme had remained unswervingly faithful to the Crown, but had been treated with ill-disguised disfavour, and such slight rewards as it obtained it owed to its connection with the Constable.

The house of Guise was a cadet branch of that of Lorraine. Of royal and French origin, on the female side, its connection with the Duchy of Lorraine caused it to be regarded as foreign to France. The Lorrainer and the foreigner became convertible terms. The Duke of Guise had endeared himself to the nation by his great services and his personal attractions, but the Cardinal's great abilities had not made him the more popular.

The rivalry was rather one of place-hunting than of principle, yet in foreign policy there had been hitherto an intelligible difference, the house of Montmorenci desiring peace and alliance with the Catholic powers, the Duke of Guise being ready to welcome Turk or heretic as allies in the struggle with Spain. The Guises had contrived the marriage of their niece, Mary Stuart, with Henry's heir, and the accession of Francis gave them the supremacy.

Thus the discomfort which resulted from the breakdown of the monarchy was attributed, as had often been the case in England, to the government of foreigners, and the exclusion of the national and constitutional advisers from the royal council. The Cardinal of Lorraine was regarded with the same hostility by Frenchmen as was the Franche-Comtois Granvelle by the nobility and townsfolk of the Netherlands. In addition to their foreign blood both Cardinals were subject to charges of ultramontane tendencies and financial maladministration. The Montmorenci party now went into open opposition, the Constable into political opposition, while the Bourbons, the Admiral, and the Cardinal Châtillon joined the religious opposition, which had already found a convert in D'Andelot. Yet outwardly the policy of uncle and nephews was yet one. Although in the provinces Catholics and Reformers were beginning to break heads, the Reformers and discontented Catholics could hardly be politically distinguished.

Early in 1560 occurred the rising named the "Tumult of Amboise." Its aims were most variously stated. Enemies said that it was intended to assassinate King and Council, and establish a Federal Republic on the Swiss model. Friends asserted that the only object was to present a petition. There seems little doubt that it was designed to remove the King from Guise's influence, and that there would have been slight scruple as to means.

The plot was betrayed, and was barbarously suppressed. It was not an exclusively Huguenot movement. Many Catholics were engaged in it, and even the Constable was suspected. It was a premature attempt. But the unpopularity caused by the brutal executions, and the open Huguenot revolt in districts of Southern France, led to the Assembly of Notables at Fontainebleau. Here the more moderate and solid minds of the Opposition, L'Hôpital and Coligni, Bishop Montluc and Archbishop Marillac, gave out-spoken expression to the general discontent, whether political or religious, while the Government took its stand on the principles of Catholicism and absolutism, for it was easy to prove that the Tumult of Amboise was an attack upon royalty by the heretical party. The King, it was urged, could summon to Council whom he pleased, and the Crown was pledged to Catholicism. The Opposition, however, was too strong to be silenced, and a meeting of the Estates General was conceded. The Government hoped to intimidate the deputies by crushing the heads of the Opposition before their organisation was complete. The Guises now, as again in 1585, deliberately attempted to remove the Bourbons from their path. Had it not been for the young King's death, Condé, and probably Navarre, would have lost their heads, and the other Bourbons were out of the question as party leaders. The backbone would have been taken from the opposition. To modern students it is clear that either panacea was but a quack remedy. Neither the expulsion of the foreigner, nor the judicial murder of the heads of the opposition, would have healed a disease too inveterate for remedial measures.

The breakdown of personal government had occurred before, and it was to occur again. The French Monarchy was a strong-growing plant, which starved all else, and finally lacked sustenance. The land required much stirring and much blood before it could once more bear it. Disorganisation of a highly organised system is the worst form of anarchy. Contemporaries, especially Italians, realized how the monarchy had deteriorated since the days of Louis XII. Machiavelli ha[s] lauded it as the model of a well-knit constitutional monarch[y] resting on its perfect system of justice which controlled t[he] Crown, while the Church advised the Crown, and a numero[us] and patriotic nobility, no longer seeking isolation, fenced round. Comines, more prophetic, had foreseen that popul[ar] control of legislation and judicature is less important tha[n] control of finance, and now we find Italian observers co[n]trasting French liberties unfavourably with those of Englan[d] under the Tudors, and Spain under Philip II. Taxation, no[t] as afterwards, had ruined the country first, and then t[he] Crown. Louis XI. had compared the kingdom to a fa[t] prairie, which he mowed at will. Maximilian likened t[he] French King to a shepherd of sheep with golden fleeces, whic[h] they allowed to be shorn at his pleasure. Francis I., whe[n] asked by Charles V. how much he took, replied, "As much a[s] I want."

The nobility which in war was the admiration of all Europ[e] in time of peace had no *raison d'être*, and no means of livin[g]. It was excluded from trade and the bar, and excluded itse[lf] from municipal employ. Either it must revolt against th[e] King, or the peasants must revolt from it. The King mu[st] make war to find employment for the nobles. The boaste[d] system of anti-feudal centralisation had broken down befo[re] the civil war began. On the one hand the magnates we[re] trying, with success, to make their provincial governmen[ts] hereditary; on the other the real rulers, the lieutenan[t] governors, were making themselves independent of bot[h] Crown and governor.

The Church had, since the Concordat, become part an[d] parcel of the monarchy, and had deteriorated with it. It ha[d] almost ceased to be a clerical body, and had entirely ceased t[o] be a constitutional body. Its revenues amounted to abou[t] one third of those of France; but they were liable to taxatio[n] almost at the King's pleasure. Benefices themselves were but form of royal revenue; it was by them that services in war, or diplomacy at court, merit in art or literature or dancing, were rewarded. Non-residence was almost universal. Benefices were dealt in, says a Venetian ambassador, like stock at Venice. Friends of Catholicism agreed that this was the chief cause of the troubles. Correr speaks of the admirable organization, the "*diligenza esquisitissima*" of the Huguenot ministers: "If our own curés had done half what they do, Christianity would not be in its present state of confusion . . . Huguenotism must go out by the same gate at which it came in; it is due to the abolition of the election of the clergy. The Concordat was the source of all evil, the non-residents and their bad substitutes."

The evil was aggravated by the indifferent character of the Papal envoys. The Florentine Tornabuoni implores his master to remonstrate with the Curia, whose greedy nuncios were hated both in France and Spain. "This country has proved how much better it would have been to send legates and nuncios who could edify than falconers of bishoprics and abbeys who have brought it to pass that the seed of Geneva and Germany has ruined the greatest kingdom of the world, with manifest danger to the rest of Christendom." (March 25, 1568.)

The judicature which Machiavelli had regarded as the safeguard of the Constitution had lost its character. This was due, writes Correr, partly to the universal practice of purchasing appointments, partly to religious prejudice. The lawyers had to pay highly for their seats, and were forced to recoup themselves by corrupt practices. It was the golden age of the French legists, but scientific jurisprudence does not necessarily imply an incorrupt judicature. The lawyers, added the Venetian, made so much money that they did not know what to do with it. Moreover, the purchase system was a temptation to the Crown to increase the number of officials, and this entailed more complication in suits, longer delay, and higher fees. Religious passion was yet more harmful to the character of the judicature. Catholic authorities testify that some judges were carried away by excess of zeal, while others could not be relied on to punish a Huguenot. Rightly or wrongly, the Parliaments no longer commanded respect.

The towns, the mercantile classes, were rich, and frequently continued rich throughout the wars. But this seemed of little benefit to the country at large. The French towns rarely had the sense of a common interest. They never formed an united estate; they were units without an unity. This separation finds expression in the vague fear, so common at the beginning of the troubles, that the towns would form themselves into separate republics. French prosperity, moreover, then as now, depended less upon urban than upon rural prosperity, and this upon *petite culture*. Sulli's maxim is of universal application, "*Labourage et paturage sont les deux mammelles de la France.*" The burden of foreign war and domestic extravagance had fallen upon the small cultivator. In Normandy and Picardy the peasants were deserting their holdings, because the profits would no longer meet the taxes. "The clergy overburdened with imposts, the nobles discontented and disunited, the people ill-affectioned"; such is the refrain of the Italian ambassadors' despatches to their Courts.

There was, then, universal demoralization and universal discontent. What was the cure? Then, as always, men said, "Revert to the past, return to the institutions which we have abandoned, reassemble the Estates General, which have had no serious meeting for eighty years, recall to the Royal Council the King's national advisers, the Princes of the Blood, restore to the Church the freedom which it occupied previous to the Concordat." *Mutatis mutandis*, the schemes for reform before the great Revolution were very similar. But in both cases the currents of thought political and spiritual had changed, the old landmarks were untrustworthy. Long ago they had proved of little service. The Gallican Church at the mercy of the nobles had been little purer than it was when at the mercy of the King. The greatest national disasters had arisen from the quarrels of the Princes of the Council. By outside observers the coming wars were attributed to this rather than to any one other cause. The feud between the great official house of Montmorenci and the house of Guise divided the country, the Council, the royal family. It was, in a Venetian's phrase, "the nursery-garden of the war." In 1560 the Florentine Envoy prophesied that civil war would break out between Guise and Montmorenci, and that this would spread into religious war. The Estates General had never shown business capacity, nor inspired respect. Their lapse had been due as much to their own inefficiency as to absolutist intention. They had been exploited before, and they would be exploited again, by royalty and revolution in turn. But the new ideas were powers pushing men knew not where, the old machinery must needs be tried, and when it failed the new forces must clash, and the result be left to apparent chance.

Condé's execution was fixed for December 10th, 1560; on December 5th the young King died from an abscess in the ear.

The death of Francis II. gave the malcontents, whether personal, political, or religious, the fairest chances of reform. For the Crown itself was in alliance with the old Opposition. Catherine di Medici had, during the last two reigns, more cause than any other to be a malcontent, and she now represented the Crown. Navarre shared the regency with her, and Condé, Montmorenci, and the Châtillons were on the same side. If the three elements, personal, political, and religious, could harmonise in government as in opposition, a radical reform seemed possible. Political reform was almost inseparable from religious, for it was based upon financial readjustment, and this upon partial disendowment and the cessation of payments to Rome. This implied a break with

Ultramontanism, a connection with Protestant powers, and a possible sympathy with the doctrinal side of the Reformation. Opposition to the clergy was distinct from attachment to Reform, but the limits as yet were far from clear. The Crown drew with it a section of the higher clergy, apart from those who, like the Cardinal Châtillon, and the Bishop of Troles, became professed Huguenots.* So closely were the religious and political aspects connected, that it was intended that a religious compromise should be effected by the Colloquy of Poissi, while deputies of the two secular estates should meanwhile decide the external form of the Gallican Church at Pontoise. Here the new ideas flowed freely. Nobles and towns demanded the exclusion of ecclesiastics from Council and all secular employ, on the ground of their cross allegiance to the Pope. The discussion of religion was referred to a National Council, pending the arrangement for a free General European Council.† Both Estates held that it was a crime to interfere with conscience, and were ready to concede liberty of worship; the Protestant assemblies should be protected by royal officers. As the Church was to be merged in the State, so the State had a right to nationalize Church property. The nobility proposed that two thirds of the State debt should be paid by the sale of Church estates, while the Third Estate advised entire resumption and a State-paid clergy,‡ part of the surplus to be applied to the extinction of the national debt, part granted on loan to the principal towns for the advancement of commerce.

The demands of the Estates were by no means exclusively religious. The extravagance of the Court was attacked, and

* Besides those mentioned, the Bishops of Aix, Valence, Pamiers, Chartres, Usez, Lescar, were summoned before the Inquisition by the Pope.

† This was a direct attack upon the legality and impartiality of the Council of Trent.

‡ Their demand for a State-paid clergy remained on the programme of the Huguenot party throughout and beyond the Wars of Religion.

retrenchment imperatively demanded. It was unfortunate for the prospects of Reform that the legislative body attacked the judicial, criticising the delay and corruption of the Law Courts, the scandalous sale of judicial and financial offices, and threatening the abolition of the newly-appointed bodies. The Parliament of Paris, which had already lost its more advanced members, turned wholly against Reform, and its irritation was increased by the contemptuous action of the Executive in not ~~subjecting~~ the Edict of Pacification for registration. The Parliament felt that in the presence of the Estates it was losing its boasted veto on legislation. The Judicature could not forget its original connection with the National Council, it would not forego its claims to legislative functions, nor be content with the special department of State consigned to it.

Immense as was the activity of the great French lawyers in jurisprudence at this period, the feverish desire to play a leading part in politics also pervaded the profession from highest to lowest. On the other hand there was a chronic dislike for the lawyers among French laymen, which, except at intermittent moments, finds no parallel in English history. The jealousy between judicature and legislature has been a prominent rock of offence in the pathway of French constitutional liberty.

More open and more immediate was the breach with the Clergy. Their conference with the Huguenot representatives, eleven ministers and twenty-two laymen, was not so harmonious as were the Estates of Pontoise. The divergences proved to be greater than had been expected, and Poissi was the watershed from which the two religions parted.

Accord being impossible, the Crown, by its edict of January, 1562, adopted the alternative of toleration. But this was more than the administration, owing to religious and political disintegration, could effect. The Crown could not quite control the higher clergy, still less could the higher clergy control the parochial curés, and the religious orders. The more eager Huguenots could not be restrained by their more prudent leaders, who counselled a waiting game. The Crown could not rely on its officials, and the officials could not secure the obedience of the people. The Parliaments desperately resisted toleration of heretical worship. Comparative harmony still existed at Court, but in the provinces the two religions were frequently at open war. At Carcassonne and Cahors Huguenots were massacred. At Nîmes, Montpellier, Montauban, and Foix, in the Cevennes and the Pyrenees, there were expulsions of priests, and wholesale iconoclasm. Huguenotism had been transformed by the addition of the fighting element, and was by no means always acting on the defensive. Religion became more and more the one absorbing topic, political reforms became subordinate, and the parties which had been acting together on political grounds began to split upon religious. War was becoming certain, and the massacre of the congregation of Vassi by the followers of the Duke of Guise was the occasion, and not the cause. It differed from a dozen other massacres only in the fact that it was committed by one of the great party leaders, and transferred the struggle from the country to the Court. The Cardinal of Lorraine at Poissi had made union impossible. His brother, the Duke, at Vassi had made war inevitable; whether his action was intentional or no it had all the effect of a fine political move, it struck the blow while Catholicism was still numerically superior, before Huguenotism had reached its full growth. Languet had written that Reform would be universal unless the Catholics provoked an immediate rupture. Nevertheless, the Huguenots were very strong, stronger than ever before or since. They all, with the one exception of Coligni, expected to win. Reform had in a measure become the national cause. Ultramontanism was the cause of the foreigner, the Guises. It was also the constitutional cause. In the Estates General of Orleans, among the nobility there had been four shades of opinion, and the extreme Huguenots had outnumbered the extreme Catholics. In the Third Estate, notwithstanding the interference of the Guise government in the elections, the Huguenots and their partisans had a large majority. The Court was known to give its sympathy, if not practical aid, to the party, and the Bench and the Bar could not have long separated themselves from it. The failure of the Huguenots and the success of the Catholics in securing the persons of the King and his mother, was rightly regarded as of momentous importance.

The different elements of which the Huguenot party was composed were strongly marked from the first. It had been long expected that any religious movement would connect itself with the old feud between Guise and Montmorenci, and between the Valois government and the discontented Bourbons.

This expectation was at once fulfilled and disappointed. The results of the Colloquy of Poissi divided each of the great discontented families. Feeling that war was inevitable, Montmorenci, who from political motives had acted with the Huguenots, cast in his lot with his own religion, while Antony of Navarre, who had carried Reformed doctrines and practices to their limits, was induced by political bribes to desert his co-religionists. Vain, unstable, indebted as he was, the loss to his party was sensible. His position as first Prince of the Blood after the royal family, his personal courage, his spendthrift generosity, the frank open manner, so often the outward sign of lack of honesty of purpose, made him the darling of the ladies, the nobility, and the troopers. Divorce from Jeanne d'Albret, with a prospect of Mary Stuart and the crown of England and Scotland, were among the bribes which tempted him. His wife remained the staunchest friend of Reform until her death in 1572. Her little kingdom of Béarn became a Huguenot principality, all Catholic priests being expelled. It formed an invaluable nucleus for the Huguenot military power, possessing as it did a small highly-trained standing army.

The real leader, however, of the Huguenots was Antony's brother Condé. An ideal chief for a discontented nobility; he had both military and political courage, a fascinating personality, and a high capacity for intrigue. His aims were probably in the main political, and his chieftainship might not improve the *morale* of his party. Yet he was more reliable than his brother, and would not desert either his political or religious associates, nor would he forswear his religious convictions, though inclined to make them subservient to his ambition. Except during his imprisonment after the battle of Dreux, he was the undoubted leader of the movement until his death at Jarnac in 1569. From the first he was accused of wishing to supplant the Valois. A medal with the inscription *Ludovicus XIII. Dei gratia Francorum rex* is said to have existed, but was believed to be a Catholic forgery. His son was a forced convert after St. Bartholomew, but escaped and served with the Huguenots until his death in 1588.* He was the favourite chief of the distinctly religious section. Yet his secretary, La Huguerye, states that he was influenced mainly by political motives. The secretary, however, became a pervert, and was not unbiassed. Among the non-royal nobility were distinguished the three Châtillon brothers. Their military or diplomatic talents, their relationship to the Constable, their burning zeal for the cause, and Coligni's† position as admiral, gave them a leading position. Of the greater nobles most perhaps stood by the Crown, but

---

* Henri Condé was very generally believed to have been poisoned by his young wife, and she was long imprisoned. The gravest doubts have existed as to the legitimacy of her posterity.

† Coligni's somewhat sullen temper made him at times a difficult colleague for his equals, but his character inspired unbounded respect among his inferiors. He was felt to be superior to personal or class considerations, and hence almost alone served to weld together the antagonistic elements of the nobles and Third Estate.

among the Huguenots were found La Rochefoucauld, the greatest man of Poitou, Rohan from Brittany, Grammont from Gascony, Montgomery, who had accidentally killed Henry II., from Normandy, the Prince of Porcian, from the Franco-Flemish frontiers. The lesser nobility flocked in large numbers from the south and west, and even from Picardy and Champagne there must have been many, judging by the force which gathered round Condé at Meaux. Yet Tavannes states that some of these were Catholics encouraged to join Condé by the queen. Montluc writes that there was scarce an honest mother's son who did not taste of heresy, especially, adds the Venetian Michiel, among those under forty. Yet Montluc's forces in the first war consisted mainly of the Catholic nobility of Guyenne. The composition of the party differed in fact infinitely according to locality. La Huguerye points out that in Languedoc few nobles were Huguenot, in Dauphiné many, while the English ambassador Smith found the gentry from Bayonne to Nantes mostly Huguenot. Of these many were zealous religionists, others disappointed soldiers, disgusted with peace and the Guises. Others were the personal adherents of the great houses, while many expected to find freedom from confession and fasting, and the discipline of a religious system whose dogma they no longer believed. All were united in common opposition to the clergy. So too in the great Albigensian movement of the south, the same rough division had been found, the bourgeois and a part of the nobility religious zealots, the majority of the nobles simply anti-sacerdotal.

The third section of Reform consisted of the upper bourgeoisie.* It was noticed that there seemed some relation between Huguenotism and success in commerce. The lower

* The Venetian Correr thus describes the motives of the several sections. The grandees adopted reform for ambition, the middle classes (the gentry) for church property, the lower classes for paradise. The latter, he adds, furnished the contributions on which the two former lived.

classes usually were faithful to their clergy, and La Noue mentions Rochelle, where the smaller people led by the ministers were more zealous than the richer citizens, as exceptional. At Toulouse a desperate struggle occurred between the Capitouls, the heads of the municipal magistracy, the upper bourgeoisie assisted by the University against the clergy, the lower magistracy, the people and the Parliament. In Normandy, the smaller people took arms against the nobles; at Dieppe it was the wealthier citizens who built a magnificent temple, at the destruction of which the populace looked on without sympathy. Marshal Tavannes states in his letters that at Dijon the common people were Catholic, and in such thoroughly Huguenot towns as Chalons and Macon he reckons the Catholics as two-thirds of the lower classes. At Troyes, the most Huguenot town of Champagne, the populace broke into the meeting-house, wrought havoc on what little furniture the Reformed service allowed, and parodied its rites.

In some few districts of France, however, whole populations rose for Reform. This was the case in the Pyrenees, and in the mountainous districts of the east of France, the Cevennes, Dauphiné, and the north of Provence.* In Guyenne occurred a rising of the peasantry, which was social and political rather than religious. Chateaux were burnt, and the peasants refused to pay either tax, tithe, or rent, and scoffingly renounced the monarchy.

Numbers are necessarily untrustworthy. In 1561 the Huguenots reckoned themselves as from 300,000 to 400,000 men, capable of bearing arms, and previous to the first war they have been stated as one-tenth of the population. This figure is probably largely exaggerated. The moderate Catholic Castelnau, writes, that it was unnecessary on the part of the

* Here the dualism between town and country stereotyped the Catholicism of the towns. Le Puy, for instance, the municipal centre of the Velai and the Vivarais, became the Catholic stronghold of the neighbourhood. The same phenomena are, *muta'is mutandis*, curiously reproduced in the great Revolution.

government to get foreign aid, for the Catholics in the first war were a hundred to one. At the close of this war the Huguenots were estimated as one-third of the nobility, and one thirtieth of the population, which seems a not unreasonable calculation.

It was of great advantage to the Huguenots that they had ample opportunities for enlisting professional soldiers. During the foreign wars the regular cavalry had become, on the evidence of a Tuscan envoy, deeply tainted with heresy.* But apart from religious sympathy, the soldiers took service where they found pay. Before the war broke out, the churches busily enrolled troops. Montluc found that all the good soldiers had joined the Huguenots, for the ministers promised not only pay but Paradise. In 1562 the ministers offered him 4,000 men to keep the peace. An old soldier of his own told him that he was captain of the Church of Nérac. "Et quel diable d'églises sont cecy, qui font les capitaines!" was the fiery old Gascon's reply. Marshal Tavannes finding that all the ablest officers had joined the Huguenots, laughed at their religious pretexts, and offered them service in the royal forces. Thus, he writes, he separated the noble from the bourgeois element, and had no more trouble; his successor neglected this method, and revolt was the result.

Geographically Huguenotism found its stronghold in the square roughly formed by the Rhone and Saône, the Loire, the Bay of Biscay, and the Pyrenees, the northern boundary running from Chalons to the mouth of the Loire. Its outlying fortresses were Normandy to the north-west, and Dauphiné to the south-east. In Normandy there was a congregation in almost every town and village. In Poitou and Guyenne in some towns the Huguenots formed a majority. At

---

* "The most deeply infected class in the whole kingdom is the Gendarmerie; it does not seem in the least likely that they can be relied on."—A. Tornabuoni, June 15th, 1560. This regular cavalry was largely composed of the poorer gentry, who served even in its lower ranks.

Rochelle Catholicism almost ceased to exist. Lower Languedoc, with its most important cities Nîmes, Montpellier, Beziers, and Castres, was in Huguenot hands; and here they fought with their backs against the parallel mountain walls which ran through the Velai, the Vivarais, and the Forez. Outside these limits Reform could obtain no firm footing. In Provence the massacre of the Vaudois had proved effective, and it was confined to the extreme north. In Burgundy and Champagne there were a few important congregations, while the Norman Huguenots kept touch with their co-religionists on the Loire by the agency of influential bodies in Maine and in Anjou. In Brittany the fact that the great nobles were for Reform was sufficient to set the people on the other side. Picardy was stoutly Catholic, and in the neighbourhood of Paris it was only found at its original seat in Meaux, and here it appears to have been endemic until the close of the wars.*

It was of momentous import that the citadel, the Vatican of Reform, was outside France, and, above all, at Geneva, for the jealousy between the two great Catholic powers guaranteed its safety. Geneva was practically a French republic, constantly recruited by raw refugee material,† and circulating in return trained ministers and money, giving unity to measures which local separations was likely to dissolve. Hence came the propagandism, the organisation for victory, the re-organisation after defeat, the *esprit de corps*, the religious zeal which

---

* How constant were the geographical proportions of Reform is found by a calculation of the number of Huguenots at the time of the Revolution of the edict of Nantes. The great square of territory described (exclusive of Lyons and Orleans) comprised 357,000 Huguenots, Normandy 50,000, and Dauphiné 75,000, whereas the numbers given for the whole of the rest of France are 133,000.

† In 1558 Geneva had, in a single day, admitted 279 foreigners to citizenship. The siege by the Duke of Savoy from 1589 to 1598 was a greater danger to Protestantism than was the siege of Paris to Catholicism. *Cf.* M. Pattison's *Casaubon*, 2nd ed., 1892, ch. ii.

whipped up flagging political or military energies. Geneva indeed preached submission, but it gave the organization and the verve which rendered resistance possible.

The first war proved that the Huguenots had miscalculated their strength. They had lost Rouen, been beaten at Dreux, and Orleans was only saved by the assassination of Guise. They had been rescued, in fact, not by their own efforts, but by the decisive mediation of the Crown. Huguenotism had been driven south of the Loire. Here it might well defend itself for a lengthened period, but it could no longer be an active aggressive power, controlling the religious and constitutional principles of the nation. To what causes was the failure due?

The apparent majority as represented in the Estates was fallacious; religious questions had been intermingled with political, with the unpopularity of the foreigner, with demands for financial reform, for more constitutional methods of government. The Estates themselves were not really representative of general opinion. The town representation was usually in the hands of the municipalities, of the upper bourgeoisie, which was frequently Huguenot, whereas the bulk of the population was Catholic. The rural classes were almost universally Catholic, rendering combined action between Huguenot centres extremely difficult. The outbreak of war and the first reverses sifted the party. The fact that the Huguenots, whether on compulsion or no, had begun the war, and the iconoclastic excesses by which the rank and file disgraced themselves, alienated the moderates hitherto inclined to tolerance. This was the class which probably decided the first three wars against the Huguenots, as it decided the final campaigns against the ultra-Catholics. It is difficult to overrate the effect of massacres, expulsions, and forced conversions. A Huguenot town once taken, a clean sweep was made of Reform. Thus Rouen and Orleans, which had been strongholds of the party in the north and centre, ended by being christened the eyes of the League. In Picardy, Champagne, and Burgundy there was hardly a Huguenot in the field by the end of the war. Heresy disappeared from most of the towns on the Loire, where it had at first been peculiarly inveterate. In Toulouse Catholic accounts report a week's massacre of 3,000 heretics, including 18 preachers.* If the Huguenots were expelled they ran every chance of being cut to pieces by the Catholic country people, among whom Catholics, worsted in civil conflict, found a refuge. It was, indeed, only in Eastern Languedoc and Dauphiné that the Huguenots solidly held their own. It was of consummate importance that the Catholics secured the two great permanent institutions of France—the Crown and the Law Courts. The Huguenots fully realised the value of the Crown, and hence Condé tried to seize the Queen-mother and the King, both before the first and the second war. All the governmental machinery was and had long been worked by the Guises. Either the provincial governers or their lieutenants were their creations. Catholic leaders, such as Tavannes in Burgundy, and Montluc in Guyenne, had all the force of legal position combined with that of personal fanaticism. Governors like Etampes in Brittany, who strove to keep the Edict, and the Comte de Tende in Provence, who protected the Huguenots, were exceptions. The bureaucracy was in favour of the Crown, on which its position depended. The Crown had command of the regular revenues, while the Huguenots were dependent on voluntary contributions. Above all, the contract with the Swiss Cantons for troops was with the Crown, and it was by pressing this point that Tavannes neutralized the action of the first Swiss troops which the Huguenot agents levied. The Parliaments had by this time completely turned against Reform. Their idea of toleration had extended only to liberty of conscience; public recognition of two forms of worship was opposed to the unity of the State, of which the

* To cast reflection upon the character of Huguenot divines, Catholic authorities stated that these 18 preachers had only 15 ears between them.

Parliaments were the guardians. Moreover, the interests of the lawyers had been threatened. They had usurped the functions of the Estates General, the revival of which filled them with jealousy and alarm; the wholesale reform of the judicature was eagerly pressed by the deputies. The fact that the Estates were on the side of the Reformation was sufficient in itself to throw the Parliaments on the side of Catholicism. There was, moreover, a jealousy of long standing between the *noblesse de robe* and the two chief elements of Huguenotism, the *noblesse d'épée*, and the *gens de commerce*. Jealousy, too, between the standing Courts of Law and the legal representative of what they regarded as the irregular judicial power of the King's Council, the Chancellor, and L' Hôpital passed for a Huguenot. The Edict of January had been registered by the Parliaments with reluctance or resistance, and they now gave the Huguenots publicly up to massacre. The Parliament of Rouen, expelled from its seat, established itself at Louviers; that of Toulouse was prominent in the annihilation of the *élite* of the bourgeoisie. Its action was so notorious, that, by the Peace of St. Germain, it was excluded from hearing any case in which Huguenots were engaged.

The Parliaments, in their own phrase, "sat upon the lilies," and were justified in refusing to leave their seat. Equally natural was the hesitation of most of the Liberal Churchmen, the diplomatists, the men of letters. Modern writers have attributed to their defection the failure of the cause. But it was the sword that turned the scale, and not the pen. Literati are too ready to think that in times of revolution the action of their predecessors was the motive power. It was in this case merely the feather which showed the direction of the wind.

The bulk of the upper classes was, as future events proved, essentially royalist in sympathy. There was in the left wing of Huguenotism a decided savour of republicanism, or of revolt from the legitimate succession. Montluc may, or may not, have been true in stating that in 1561 the Huguenots of Guyenne debated the replacement of the Valois by a "*roi des fidèles.*" It is certain that the first outbreak was disgraced by anti-royalist excesses. The head of Francis II. was broken into dust, and thrown into the river at Orleans. The bones of Louis XI. at Notre Dame de Clery were given to the dogs, while at Angoulême the sepulchres of the ancestors of Francis I. were desecrated.

Of the importance of Paris to the Catholic cause it will be well to speak elsewhere. Suffice it to say here that it was fully realized by all the Huguenot leaders. It was directly or indirectly the object of all Coligni's or Navarre's attacks. Either they would move on the town itself, or they would starve it out by the possession of its food avenues, Normandy and the lower Seine, or the streams which flowed from eastward and southward into the Parisian basin.

Finally the Huguenot party was not sufficiently organized nor sufficiently homogeneous. As soon as the war broke out jealousy appeared between the noble and the bourgeois elements, and between the religious and the secular. Tavannes states that in 1563 he saw letters from Geneva to the towns, warning them to trust to the nobility. Calvinism was equally intolerant with Catholicism, and more self-sufficient. The disciples of toleration, and the libertines who had left Catholicism on account of the severity of its discipline, found that they had changed for the worse. With many the new doctrines had signified merely a revolt against the clergy; it was no gain to pass from the domination of the priest to that of the minister.

The Huguenot nobility were excellent military material, but were not yet an army. They went lightly into the war, as they raced helter-skelter into Orleans, and many went lightly out of it. Condé had to disperse the bulk of his forces after he had taken Orleans. He could not keep them in the field. Many were poor, their families were in real danger, their interests were provincial.

It was long before they formed a thoroughly reliable force. Their want of discipline lost Jarnac, their inconsiderate eagerness to fight lost Moncontour. The issues of the war depended mainly on the following of the chiefs, and were decided far away from the Huguenot civic centres. The nobility only were found in the first line; the townspeople were fully occupied with local warfare. From abroad the Catholics received more aid than the Huguenots. The Spanish auxiliaries were more valuable than the English, and at this time more disinterested.

It was a shock to the national conscience that the Huguenot chiefs had handed Havre and Dieppe to the old national enemy; it was well known that the English price was the recovery of Calais. The Calvinism of the Huguenots barred to them the mercenary resources of the greater part of Germany. If a Palatine prince raised reiters for their service, a Saxon prince levied his Lutherans for the Crown. Throughout the wars no German Catholic fought in the Calvinist lines, but the Catholic agents recruited freely from Protestant states. The great recruiting-sergeant of the French Crown, Schomberg, was himself a Protestant.

The first war decided, once and for all, that France should not be a Protestant nation. How was it that the two next did not decide its exclusive Catholicism? In the second war the Huguenots rather gained than lost. They were strong enough to besiege Paris, to get the better in a battle outside its walls. The third peace was yet more favourable than the first and second, notwithstanding the defeats of Jarnac and Moncontour. This was due, in some degree, to the altered condition of the party; other causes, and perhaps the more weighty, were external.

In the two latter wars the light-heartedness had disappeared; the party was purged of its less satisfactory elements, it was now a matter of grim earnest, of life and death. Technically the Huguenots again took the offensive, but even if, as seems probable, they were mistaken, they had every reason to fear surprise.

The Venetian ambassador, Correr, believes that in 1566 they only anticipated attack, and so unimpeachable an authority as Marshal Tavannes explicitly states this of 1568. The Huguenots were now more concentrated in their own provinces of the south-east and south-west. The towns which had remained Huguenot were the most stubborn, and had been reinforced by the exiles from other congregations. The royal armies broke themselves again and again against their walls. The resistance of St. Jean d'Angeli after Moncontour probably saved the cause. Undisciplined as they still were, the small fighting nobility were after all the flower of France; they were well horsed, and had great rapidity of movement. The Turkish envoy, who was no mean critic, spoke in terms of unqualified praise of their conduct at St. Denis.*

The Moderates even before St. Bartholomew were swinging back to the weaker party. The Constable's death at St. Denis, as will be seen, contributed to this. The professional soldiers, such as Vielleville and Cossé, detested the mutual throat-cutting for the benefit of Spaniards and Lorrainers. When Vielleville was asked who won the battle of St. Denis he replied, "The king of Spain."

In the Catholic ranks there was a general unwillingness to fight. L'Hôpital vouches for the jealousies and divisions in the royal camp. The Crown was unwilling to push matters to extremities; the state of its finances rendered the continuance of war impossible, unless it would accept the proffered subsidies of Philip and of Paris. But a more decisive cause was the revolt in the Netherlands. Cateau Cambrésis had turned attention inwards. The rising of the Gueux turned it again outwards.

Could France let slip the opportunity of reverting to the

---

* The operations of seven small potentates of Southern France, familiarly termed the Viscounts, are well worthy of a military monograph.

anti-Spanish policy, the abandonment of which had caused all her troubles? Could she suffer her fighting material to be annihilated when the losses of Francis I. might be recovered?

"We always won by arms," wrote the Catholic Gascon Montluc, "they by those confounded writings." He attributes the excellent terms which the Huguenots obtained at the second Peace to their influence on the Royal Council. The Council indeed could not adopt a purely sectarian attitude.

The Huguenot leaders used the advantages offered by the Peace of St. Germain to the full. They hoped once more to control the Crown, as they had hoped to control it on the death of Francis II.

Coligni's personality stamped itself on the impressionable imagination of the young King. The union between the Catholic Crown and the Huguenot Princes of the Blood was to be cemented by the marriage of the king's sister with Henry of Navarre, son of Jeanne d'Albret, the staunchest and stiffest of Calvinist ladies. The result would be immediate war upon Spain, a war national and political, but entailing, as all Catholics saw, the triumph of Reform in both France and the Low Countries.

Tavannes, not unjustly from the ultra-Catholic point of view, describes the stages of the Huguenot revolt.

(1) It was stimulated by Catherine di Medici, in order to strengthen her position and eject the Guises. (2) The Huguenots themselves expected to control King and State. (3) They were compelled to fight for bare life. (4) They were slaughtered at St. Bartholemew for wishing to force the Catholics to take up their quarrel against Spain, and suffer all the loss, while the Huguenots would harvest the gains.

That the Catholics would be forced into the Spanish war seemed certain, for they had lost their leaders, and could offer no organized resistance, while the Moderates were only too willing to wipe their blood-stained swords on Spanish bodies. But it was at this crisis that the loss of Condé was appreciably felt. His undoubted position, his gaiety and courtesy, the absence of religious exclusiveness, his favour with Catherine, all these qualities might, in the temporary obscurity of the House of Guise, have won the Catholic nobility to a war which, in his hands, would have assumed a less religious complexion.

Coligni, soldier and statesman as he was, was no diplomat. He had acquired somewhat of the masterful roughness of his creed. He was too uncompromising to conceal his feelings; above all, he could not get on with women. His inconsiderate monopoly of her son now wounded Catherine in her tenderest point. Thus the final tragedy had, as might have been expected, its political and its religious side. The resolve of the Queen to free the crown from the great official who controlled it was combined with the feud between Guises and the Huguenot branch of the Montmorenci, and with the hatred of the Parisian democracy for the nobilty of Southern France.

St. Bartholemew was, in a measure, the re-enactment of the great Armagnac slaughter, which preceded the English war. The Parisian bourgeois believed that he had been freed, not only from heresy, but from a feudal reaction, and curiously the Catholic noble of Northern France believed that his country had been saved a disruptive and republican Federalism which would have taken the Swiss Confederacy for its model.

These beliefs, apparently contradictory, have been continuously transmitted to Catholic writers of modern days. It will be worth while therefore, before proceeding to the second stage of the Religious Wars, to consider the first of these accusations, while the second will be more conveniently treated hereafter.

The question of a feudal reaction can be best tested by a reference to the demands of the Estates of Orleans, and the Deputation of Pontoise, which apparently had Huguenot majorities, to the manifesto of Condé (which gave the professed object of the war), and to the concessions claimed in the Peaces which terminated the three first wars.

The conclusion of such an enquiry will probably be, that this period shows an all round reaction against the pressure of modern monarchy. Every organization that had, to all appearance, been stifled or absorbed, gave signs of fresh and independent life. The Church cried for the revival of Gallican liberties, for National Councils, for the replacement of the Concordat by the Pragmatic Sanction. The Estates General demanded periodical sittings, control over taxation, the subordination of the Judicature, municipal liberties. Among such demands feudal elements naturally reappeared. The nobility demanded baronial jurisdiction, as did the bourgeoisie municipal. They claimed the exclusive right of hunting, a sharper line between noble and *roturier*.

Such claims are more or less feudal, and were pressed by nobles more or less Huguenot. But the Third Estate, also more or less Huguenot, made demands of a distinctly anti-feudal character, protection for the peasant against oppressive *corvées* and cruel usage, against the abuses of such seignorial jurisdiction as remained, the intervention of royal judicial officers between the lord and his subjects.

Thus there was no precise coincidence between Huguenotism and Feudalism. Many or most of the same demands were made in the Estates General of the League.

The objects of Condé's manifesto, and of the three Peaces, are partly political, partly religious; on the one hand the liberation of the king from a clique of foreign favourites, and the restoration of the Princes of the Blood to their proper influence; on the other, the toleration accorded by the Edict of January. Here the political object is not feudal; it is not independence but influence; it is to bring the princes nearer to, not to take them further from, the Crown. Condé and his partisans insisted on rehabilitation, on recognition that they had acted loyally in the Crown's interest. They never had regarded themselves as fighting against the Crown. The King, they held, was an involuntary prisoner in the hands of the Lorrainer.

But, curiously enough, it is from the religious side that the feudal element emerges. The strongest restriction is imposed upon the worship of the non-feudal element. The right of the burghers to differ from the king's religion is a matter not of class, but of local privilege. The noble in his castle may do as he pleases, he is to be as religiously independent as he was of old judicially and politically. The nobles had here been the gainers, they had made the most show in the wars, and had the making of the peace. Thus but for St. Bartholomew it is possible that the wars might have favoured a return towards Feudalism. As Feudalism had been based in the past partly on decentralisation of justice, partly on decentralisation of military service, so now it might have found a new foundation in decentralisation of religion. In Germany this had been the case. The principle, *Cujus regio, ejus religio*, had been the last word of feudalism.

The Venetian Barbaro compared the Bourbons leading the Huguenots for political reasons against the Guises, to the German houses leading the Lutherans against the House of Hapsburg. Reform had been brought to the fighting point by the discontent of the military classes. It was natural that peace should depend on their contentment.

The power of the Huguenots was profoundly modified by the great massacre. It was criticised at the time as being perhaps a crime, but certainly a blunder; the number of the slain was either too many or too few. Tavannes, however, points out, that whereas, notwithstanding the defeats of Jarnac and Moncontour, the Huguenots could previously keep the field, they could never, after 1572, bring an army into action unless aided by the Catholics of South France.

Catholic writers of recent years have thought it worth while to minimise the number of the victims of St. Bartholomew.

If, however, to those killed at Paris be added those who were slaughtered in the provinces, the total is very considerable.* But it is no matter of counting noses. The massacre cut off the dominant element of the Huguenots, the fighting, aggressive class, the class which necessarily had political influence. Those who were killed at Paris were the more important, the more adventurous, both militarily and politically. The party as a whole, and each province separately, lost its natural leaders. Coligni was never replaced. The Huguenots never again possessed a leader in whom his great military qualities, his high official position, his prudence, and his steadfastness were combined.† That Navarre and Condé were forced to pervert was perhaps more injurious than their death. It was a bad example. Many of the Huguenot nobility, whose religion had throughout been somewhat colourless, definitely reverted to Catholicism.‡ The remainder were scattered, disabled for combined action. On the other hand the bourgeois element in the towns and districts where it had been strongest was intact. The result was a complete transformation of the party. The ministers and the bourgeois and the lesser local gentry assumed the lead, the purely

* The numbers slain in Paris were variously computed from 10,000 to 1,000, the latter figure being probably more correct. But to this figure provincial massacres would add at least 10,000. For information on the Massacre, see *North British Review*, October, 1869 (Lord Acton); *Proceedings of the Huguenot Society*, January, 1887, (Sir H. Austen Layard); and the Cte. de la Ferrière's *Avant et après le St. Barthélemy*, 1892.

† The loss, indeed, was not only that of the party, but of the nation. France has, perhaps, never reproduced the type of Coligni and Teligni. No nation can afford to ostracise or massacre the flower of its nobility. Of all the excuses and explanations for the agony of 1870, "C'est le St. Barthélemy qui nous tue aujourdhuy" was possibly the truest.

‡ Priuli, writing in 1582, states that Huguenotism had decreased by 70 per cent. He dwells also on the religious indifference of the higher classes in France, as contrasted with the fervent, if somewhat exoteric, zeal of the lower. His remarks are applied to the Catholic party, but are probably true of both.

religious element was forced to the front, for it was for religious existence, not for political control, that the struggle was continued.

The fourth war was no longer a war of movement, of forced marches by noble cavalry, but essentially a war of sieges. The unity of the party had hitherto consisted in the persons of the great leaders. This it was now attempted to replace by a representative federal system, by utilising to the full for defensive purposes the machinery which the Congregational system suggested or supplied. It may almost be said that the ministers took the place of the nobles, and that they substituted for a military aristocracy a democratic theocracy. The organization proposed in a synod at Béarn is practically a federal republic. Each town should annually elect a mayor for military and civil command, and two councils of twenty-four and sixty-five members respectively for legislation, coinage, taxation, the decision in peace and war. The mayors and councils should elect a general chief and council for the province on a similar model. In 1573 this suggestion was adopted in the Estates of the party at Nîmes and Montauban. Languedoc and Upper Guyenne formed two governments, each with its elective chief acting under the control of the Estates. Within the Government each diocese held its separate Estates. It was determined to sequestrate all ecclesiastical property, to levy taxation on Huguenots and Catholics alike. More than this, the system was to be extended over the whole of France, with the progress of Reform.

Here was Revolution. The governmental system of the country was entirely set aside, and a party, non-official organization substituted for it. Nor was the practice without its theory. It was no longer possible to pretend that the Huguenots were fighting for the Crown, that the Queen-mother and her son were in durance vile, and must be delivered. It is possible that from the first revolutionary theories had existed among the townspeople and the ministers, but the official programme of the party was eminently loyal. The Synod of La Ferté sous Jouarre had indeed been accused of an approach to the revolutionary doctrine of the Dominion of Grace, of holding that all the magistrates in France had forfeited their office by sin, and were no true magistrates. This accusation, however, had been indignantly and authoritatively denied. Political pamphlets had originally been mere personal invectives, directed against the House of Guise, and the improper influence of foreigners. But the foreigner is now not the Lorrainer, but the Italian, that is, the Queen-mother. The Genevan preacher had little respect for the King, and less for his mother. From the days of Knox the maladministration of women had been a favourite theme with the ministers. Hence the massacre was followed by a swarm of political pamphlets, some mere passing satires, others of permanent interest in the history of political thought. Models were ready to hand in the *brochures* directed by the Marian exiles against the Catholic government. Of these pamphlets, the two most remarkable are the *Franco Gallia* of Hotman, and the *Vindiciæ Contra Tyrfaños*, by Languet or Du Plessis Mornay. The former, adopting the historical method, attempts to prove that the absolutism of the monarchy was a breach in the continuity of French history, that its true basis was a nation of freemen with an elective and constitutional monarchy, that the fountains of freedom, Gallic and Teutonic, had been tainted by the influx of Italian ideas, Roman domination, Imperial law, Italian women and politicians; France, to be free, must revert to the original principles, the official elective kingship, the national Estates, the exclusion of the women and the foreigner. The *Vindiciæ*, on the other hand, arguing on the deductive method, adopts as its postulate an original compact between king and people. Each contracting party had its engagements to fulfil, and the Crown, from its failure to execute the contract, had released the people from its obedience. These books are merely, however, good examples of a considerable literature, in which the same arguments, the same illustrations, frequently the same words reappear.* It is important to observe that these pamphlets almost exclusively belong to the years between 1572 and 1576, by which time, as will be seen, the party was again transformed.

There was probably no moment when Huguenot was so sharply distinguished from Catholic as during the short period which elapsed between St. Bartholomew and the Treaty of Rochelle. There could be no common bond to tie together the shattered and scattered relics of the party but religion. It offered no scope for the ambitious, no redress for the malcontent. Resistance was confined to isolated localities. The existence of Huguenotism as a political element in the State seemed to be closed. Yet, within two years from the Treaty of Rochelle, the party was more political and more powerful than ever, and in 1576 extracted the extraordinarily favourable Peace of Monsieur, which may be regarded as the high-water mark of Huguenot success. This sudden turn of fortune was due to two causes of an almost exclusively political character—the union with the Politiques of the South of France, and the re-union with the Princes of the Blood.

The former was closely connected with the family factions of the reign of Henry II. The expectation that any religious conflict would become merged in the feud between the houses of Guise and Montmorenci had been deceived owing to the zealous Catholicism of the Constable, which at the last moment caused his alliance with his enemy. Yet the breach with the Guises was never closed, the old Constable was more than once on the point of breaking from them, his son, the Marshal, Governor of Paris, fired upon the Cardinal of Lorraine when he entered with an escort, and was consistently just in

* I have treated this subject at length in the *English Historical Review* 1889.

his dealings towards the Huguenots. After the death of the Constable at St. Denis the breach became complete. The Marshal was in 1574 imprisoned, and in danger of his head, for complicity with the malcontent Princes of the Blood. The two youngest brothers became active Huguenots, while Marshal Damville, Governor of Languedoc, became in effect king of Southern France, ruling alike over Catholic and Huguenot.

The Politiques were, in the happy phrase of their enemy Tavannes, "those who preferred the repose of the kingdom or their own homes to the salvation of their souls; who would rather that the kingdom remained at peace without God, than at war for Him." There were naturally Politiques throughout the length and breadth of France, but they only became an organized party in the South, precisely there where the two creeds had been most evenly balanced, and most closely intermingled, where passions had been hottest, where blood had flowed most freely. It was here that the continuance of the war had become intolerable, and the Southern Catholics were perhaps horrified at a crime in which they had not shared.* Of such a party Marshal Damville, himself a Catholic, but the opponent of the Catholic leaders, was the natural head. As early as 1573 the Politiques of Poitou are found sending deputies to a Huguenot assembly. But in 1574 the Politiques of Languedoc, under Damville, formed a definite alliance, and in 1575, at the great assembly of Nîmes, a regular Constitution was drawn up for the union of the two parties. Damville, in the absence of Condé, appointed head of the Huguenots as well as of the Politiques, or, as they called themselves, the Peaceable Catholics. The districts affected were administered in complete independence of the Crown—

* To this was attributed the conversion of the young Vte. de Turenne to Protestantism, a gain which counterbalanced many losses; for, apart from his talents, his estates lying in the centre of Southern France, helped to connect the western, southern, and eastern sections of the Huguenots.

Estates were annually held and taxes collected. These latter the administration professed to be willing to hand over to the Crown as soon as political reform was inaugurated, and political grievances redressed. It was constantly reported that this district was more regularly administered and more lightly taxed than any part of royalist France. It is clear, however, that the objects of this League were purely defensive, its character strictly local, and its tendencies separatist. It is to be reckoned among the many instances of the non-homogeneity of the South of France.

The condition of affairs was materially altered by the escape of the Princes of the Blood. A movement which had as its chiefs Condé, Henry of Navarre, and Alençon, the King's brother and heir presumptive, must necessarily affect the whole kingdom. The party, indeed, took the offensive with the aid of John Casimir and his Palatinate *reiters*. To him was promised first the possession, and then the occupation of the three Bishoprics, the important acquisition of Henry II. Thus again the Huguenot party was disgraced by the incurable tendency of the great nobles to seek foreign aid in revolt against the Crown at the expense of the national territory. The terms wrung from the Queen-mother included the surrender of the Governorship of Picardy, a stout Catholic province, to Condé, which would at last bring the French Calvinists into touch with their co-religionists in the Netherlands. The treaty provoked a sharp Catholic reaction; so sharp indeed that Damville and the Southern Politiques, who regarded the offensive Huguenot action as a breach of faith, were for a moment found upon the royalist side.* The war was, however, but of a moment's duration, and the peace of Bergerac was patched up to leave Alençon's hands free for his Netherland adventures. The period which lies between this

* On the one hand the Crown used every effort to win Damville, on the other the Huguenots injudiciously threatened him, accusing him both of religious favouritism and political absolutism.

and the outbreak of the League has a very peculiar character, and does little credit to the Huguenot party, or at least to its leaders. Personal considerations and court intrigue take the place of religious zeal. Henry of Navarre and Condé were too jealous to act in concert, and the stricter Huguenots looked to the latter as their leader, suspecting, not without reason, the genuineness or permanency of Henry's re-conversion. Many others believed that a very tolerable *modus vivendi* had been disturbed by the intrusion of the Princes of the Blood, and looked to Damville as their constitutional leader, Catholic as he was. They refused to take part in the Lovers' War, which they regarded as unwarrantable aggression adopted for improper personal motives. Religious zeal seemed to have burnt itself out, and there were signs that the religious parties would give place to fresh combinations, based on personal or constitutional affinities. Henry of Navarre was drawing near to the king; Condé to Alençon. The gallant Huguenot Captain, La Noue, proposed that all mention of religious differences should be dropped, and that Huguenots and Catholics should combine in an attack upon the abuses of the royal administration. It was not merely the moderates who were disposed to combine for the peace and reform of the nation, but mysterious agents were constantly on the move between the extreme left-wings of the two religions, the houses of Guise and Condé. In these intrigues John Casimir was concerned, and there were grounds for believing that they might result in a sudden attack upon the Crown, or that both parties, ashamed of the brutalities of civil war, might strive to forget the past in an onslaught upon the weaker neighbours of France along the Rhine. But the most peculiar phenomenon of this period is to be found in the strongly Protestant province of Dauphiné. This, it will be remembered, was one of the few districts where the lower classes were devoted to Reform. But here the religious conflict had given place to, or become merged in, a social conflict. The people became imperceptibly engaged in a desperate struggle against the gentry, in which religious distinctions seem to have dropped entirely out of sight, and the people, Huguenot as in the main they were, received support from the house of Guise, disposed at this time to rely upon the masses, of whatever creed.

It seemed not unlikely that this social war might spread over France. The Venetian Badoer, writing in 1582, regarded the hostility between nobles and people as of more importance than religious differences. The causes which he assigns are of permanent weight, and form one of the many interesting links between the Wars of Religion and the Revolution. "There is extremely bad feeling between nobles and people, who are much oppressed by the large quantities of poor gentry, who play the tyrant, and expect to live, dress, and take their pleasure at the people's expense. This lawlessness of the nobles has enormously increased, especially in places distant from the Court, and there is little hope of remedy, for these poor gentlemen are, owing to the eldest son inheriting the greater portion of the family property, forced to live in this way. Partly the means of supporting themselves in the gendarmerie has failed them, for this force no longer receives pay; partly they have become accustomed in the civil war to live with much license and extravagance on the shoulders of the poor."

Had Alençon succeeded to the throne, or had Henry of Navarre earlier abjured his professed faith, the Wars of Religion might have died a natural death. As it was, the somewhat sudden death of Alençon produced a startling change. Henry III.'s life was notoriously a bad one, and he had no hope of issue. Henry of Navarre was heir presumptive, and the sense of Catholic France revolted against a heretic king. Keen observers even now recognized that his ultimate acceptance of Catholicism was a certainty, but if not too spiritual he was at least too spirited to be converted at dictation. Hence the great Catholic uprising, which will be treated hereafter. The first effect of this was to rally Huguenots of whatever class, and of whatever principles, round him who was now their natural leader. It might be expected that the dividing line would once more be purely religious, that the political aspect of the movement would be at least obscured. Yet this was far from the case. It was recognized that the Catholic League implied not merely the suppression of heresy, but the extinction of the house of Bourbon in favour of the house of Guise. Hence Damville and his southern Politiques were almost without hesitation on Henry's side. The King himself, and the handful of professional soldiers who adhered to him, were known to resent his exclusion from succession. The Catholic members of the house of Condé, Soissons and Conti, fled to join Navarre, and the old Duke of Montpensier, nothwithstanding the influence of his beautiful virago, Catherine of Guise, was avowedly opposed to the action of his wife's house. A large proportion of the nobility in the centre and south declared for the Bourbons. This added enormously to the mobility of the party, to its power of taking the offensive, yet it also accentuated internal difficulties of long standing. The ministers and citizens, who for a moment after St. Bartholomew had almost monopolized resistance, were disinclined to be once more ousted by the noble element, whose religion was of a somewhat shifting hue. Nor did they ever thoroughly trust Navarre. It was fortunate for him that his rival, Condé, was removed in 1588. It is true that the Huguenot political theory was forced to execute a complete *volte face*. The fundamental character of the Salic Law of legitimate succession was now enforced by press and pulpit, with as much energy as had been the original compact, and the right of deposition. But in practice the Republican Federalist spirit survived. It showed itself at the great assembly of Rochelle in 1588. There were protests against over-centralisation, against the tyrannical protectorate. It was demanded that each province should have its separate protector. Henry felt the pulse of his party and anticipated the federalist scheme. He insisted that he would only be president by virtue of election. He instituted provincial chambers of justice to check his officers, and a controlling council of twelve members, his Chancellor, six elected annually by the provinces (Upper and Lower Languedoc, Dauphiné, Guyenne, Poitou, Rochelle), and five by the General Assembly every other year. The united Catholic party was invited to adopt a parallel constitution. Every governor of province or town was subjected to a similar check. The bourgeois held the purse, and they meant to hold the reins. Constitutional questions were forced into the background by the tragedies of 1588 and 1589, by the constant military movement now of an essentially offensive character, by the fact that the murder of Henry III. gave Navarre a position which it would be suicidal for his party to deny. Yet, that the old class jealousies subsisted is proved by the later history of the Huguenot party.

The last act of Huguenotism as a political element opens with the recognition of Henry as king of France by the bulk of the Catholic party, and with his reconciliation with his Papacy. Henry's gain was the Huguenot loss. The resistance of the ultra-Catholics he had partly fought down and partly bought out. But the bribes had consisted in religious as well as in pecuniary engagements. Leaguer towns and governors had pledged him to the exclusion of Huguenot worship from the area of their influence; whereas in the early war Huguenot defeats had led to the expansion of their privileges, their final victory appeared to threaten shrinkage. Even before the King's abjuration, the party had threatened to look elsewhere for a Protector; it had negotiated independently with England and Holland. After the abjuration, the first formal demand of the southern Huguenots was, that they should be allowed to choose both a foreign and a native Protector. This was to give a foreign prince a recognised right of interference in French politics, and a native prince the right of revolt against the crown. The party was profoundly disaffected. It disliked the King's ideal of a Gallican patriarchate, of a scheme of unity which would act as a solvent of the party organization, and water down its doctrines. The more religious section comprising such men as d'Aubigné, was scandalized at the divorce, at the King's obvious desire to place his mistress on the throne. The political section, headed by Bouillon and La Trémouille aimed at securing provincial independence or national importance, by utilising the organization which the King had neither the power nor the will to break. The obvious danger wrung from the Council a re-enactment of the favourable Edict of 1577. But the Huguenots were again becoming a separatist anti-governmental party. They threatened to renounce governmental guarantees, to re-organize their military and financial system, and to occupy their strong places in defiance of the Court. The nation's misfortune was their opportunity. Open war with Spain had followed Henry's recognition, and the Spaniards had surprised Amiens and were astride upon the Somme. The more royalist section of the Huguenots, headed by Mornay, would give aid to the King, and trust to his liberality, but the bulk of the party held back, and few marched to the recovery of Amiens. The extremists wished even to seize Tours and to hold the Loire as the Spanish held the Somme. But Henry's success, the peace with Spain, the submission of the last Leaguer stronghold in Brittany, convinced the Huguenots of the danger of isolation. Hence the Edict of Nantes, which was to permanently regulate the relations of the two parties, to be the standard of reference in France, as the Peace of Augsburg was in Germany. Catholicism was henceforth the State religion; it was universal, where it had ceased to exist it was restored; it recovered its lost estates, its tithes. But to the Huguenots liberty of conscience was universally conceded, and extensive local privileges as to liberty of worship. On the political side, they demanded three guarantees for their security: (1) places of security; (2) the right of holding royal offices; (3) a proportion of members in the Courts of Justice. Thus only could they be protected from surprise, from political nonentity, and from judicial persecution.

The Edict of Nantes was no general legalization of toleration. It did not admit the principle that a citizen's form of worship was indifferent to the State. It was rather a treaty between two powers comparatively equal. Privileges were accorded to a certain class generally, and to certain localities individually. Huguenotism was not absorbed in the State system. Nay, rather its independence was accentuated. Even in Henry's lifetime the pseudo-feudal element had to receive a lesson in the punishment accorded to Turenne, now Duke of Bouillon. Yet it was far from extinct, and was dangerous from the support which it might draw from religious associations. The municipal element had all the sturdiness of long years of independent administration. Moreover, in the south, Huguenotism possessed a large measure of local solidarity. In this party the representative element was long lived. While the estates of the realm dropped into disuse, those of the Huguenots were regularly held every three years, consisting of thirty gentlemen, twenty ministers and ten members of the third estate. Their deputies watched their interests at Court, their agents acted as ambassadors with foreign powers. The Spaniards treated with them separately, offering them Dauphiné and the south and west of the Loire as an independent state. With their eight strong towns, and their garrison of 4,000 men, they possessed a force which was independent of the Crown, even though partly paid by it. But their danger lay in the dualism between the noble and the municipal elements, between the political and the religious. Moreover, their privileges were held in the teeth of the majority of the nation; they depended upon a strong king, who subsidised their ministers, and paid their garrisons; their continuance was only secure until a monarch arose who had the will and the power to withdraw them. Richelieu had the power to terminate the political existence of the party, and Louis XIV. the will to proscribe its religion.

II.

THE LEAGUE

WHEN the religious struggle broke out Catholicism had, in point of dead-weight, the undoubted advantage. Its divisions, its disorganization and demoralisation, could alone have given the Huguenots a reasonable hope of victory. The Church was, in the phrase of Tavannes, like a nation which had been long at peace, and which had no generals; necessity gave her leaders.

Finding the Crown inactive or unsympathetic the old religion gradually learnt to place its confidence in the house of Guise. The fortunes of French Catholicism were wedded to those of a family scarcely French. Claude of Guise, the second son of René, Duke of Lorraine, had, after the great disaster of Paris, beaten back the German advance on the eastward, and in all probability saved Paris from the English. His six sons were all richly endowed in France. The eldest was closely connected with the Crown by his marriage to the daughter of Renée, Duchess of Ferrara, and granddaughter of Louis XII. His one daughter was married to James V. of Scotland, and their child to King Henry's son Francis.

The family held three Duchy peerages, and wore two Cardinal's hats. Already under Francis I. they were jostling for power with the Montmorencis, and had shouldered out the Bourbons; already they posed as leaders of the ultra-Catholics.

It was in the family Duchy of Lorraine that the first

Reformers of French race were brought to the stake. Francis I., before his death, is said to have distrusted them as dangerous to monarchy. The women were as fascinating and as capable as the men. Mary, Regent of Scotland, Mary Stuart, and Catherine, Duchess of Montpensier, may be regarded as the three stars among the ladies of the Catholic reaction.

The defence of Metz and the capture of Calais by Duke Francis had made him the first man in France. He represented the anti-Imperial war policy, holding out a hand to the Papacy on the one hand, and to German Protestants on the other. He hoped with the Pope's aid to realize, at the expense of Spain, the old pretensions of his house to the kingdom of Naples. His ambitions were to be served by foreign war, and Spain and the Emperor were the natural enemies. Thus, zealous Catholic as he was, he would welcome the aid of foreign Protestants. It was the natural policy of France, that to which Henry IV. returned.

Courageous in action, in policy Duke Francis was lethargic, if not timid. This deficiency was supplied by his brother, the Cardinal of Lorraine, who was at once fearless in design, and physically a coward. Sceptical, or at least indifferent, he made religion the pathway to his ambition, combatting the Reformers with their own weapons, utilising the new learning in the service of the Catholic reaction, professing appreciation of Reform, that he might penetrate its secrets, skilfully widening the gap which separated Lutheranism from Calvinism. His aim was to stand at the head of a revived Catholicism, to be spread by Spanish arms and Spanish fires. Here then he and his brother parted company. The Cardinal joined Montmorenci in the pressure put upon the King for the Treaty of Cateau Cambrésis. National was to be exchanged for religious war.

The Duke was indignant, but it was the key to the Guise policy of the future—religious unity at the expense of national dismemberment. This was the work of the one member of the Guise family who probably had no religion. Yet the Cardinal did not realize its full effects. He was rather a diplomat than a statesman. His eloquence secured his immediate ends; he had not foresight of their ultimate results.

The House of Guise had many advantages, and some drawbacks. The family possessions lay on the borderland of France, the Spanish Netherlands, and the Empire. Lorraine cut the Spanish possessions in half, separating Franche Comté from the Low Countries. It was on the regular line of march from France to Germany, and was a convenient recruiting ground for German mercenaries. The Guises had French possessions; they could pose as representatives of the nobility, as having rights as against the Crown, claims to the great offices and governments; or they could fall back on their position as foreigners, disclaim responsibilities and duties, levy war upon the King, with a lesser show of treason. The Crown had reasons for favouring them; they were made by itself, and could, to all appearance, be unmade; they had no strong inherited provincial backing. Jealous of the lords of the lilies, the monarchy liked to balance the old French nobility by foreign importations. Thus the Duchy of Nemours had been given to a Savoyard; the Duchy of Nevers was in the hands of a Gonzaga. The Strozzi and the Gondi were also on the rise.

On the other hand, there was much dislike of this mushroom Court nobility, which was ousting the Princes of the Blood, and this set many of the Catholic orthodox nobility against the Guises. The Parliament of Paris refused to recognise them as Princes. There was general discontent that the foreigners, "the Lorraines," should occupy the benefices and great offices of France. Shortly before the outbreak of war the Catholic Parisians, on whom the power of Guise ultimately rested, attacked their urban and surburban palaces. Granvelle, watching French politics from the Netherlands, as early as 1558 told the Cardinal that they could not stand alone, that they must find friends abroad. Consequently they acted as foreigners, and found support in foreign aid. But this would not have been enough. They had no nationality, and could not head a national movement, and so they threw themselves at the head of the religious movement. When the national feeling revived they necessarily fell.

It is improbable that the Guises began with any idea of the Crown; but it is certain that they ended at reaching towards it, though they were afraid to grasp it. Yet as early as 1560 the Huguenots accused the Duke of aiming at the throne. Tavannes relates that the Queen-mother told his father that she issued the Edict of Toleration for fear of the Guises, who were aspiring to the throne. But it was impossible then, and the Duke was too practical to aim at the impossible. His ambition was under Henry II. by military fame to occupy the first place under the Crown, under Francis II. to monopolise the State by help of the Crown, under Charles IX. to domineer over both State and Crown by means of an organisation formed outside of the Crown circle. How impossible an attempt on the throne was is proved by the universal discontent, by the wide ramifications of the affair of Amboise. The Guises felt that the control was slipping from their hands; they must recover their monopoly by the annihilation of the rival houses, then they would have packed the Estates, and ruled through them, then they might have aspired to the succession of the Valois. Condé was on his trial, Coligni and Navarre in their hands, when Francis II. died, and the control of the State through the Crown must cease. It was then that the Duke accepted his brother's ideas of seeking a power outside the Crown, of leading the French Catholics in alliance with the European Catholic system, of using this organisation, if necessary, in disobedience to the Crown. This entailed reconciliation with the orthodox Catholics like Montmorenci, even in the face of long-standing personal hostility, alliance with Spain against all previous foreign feeling. The massacre of Vassi committed him to the cause, the capture of the Constable at Dreux, the deaths of S. André and Navarre, gave him the sole command of the cause, and his murder at Orleans consecrated his family to the cause.

It was of undoubted service to Catholicism to have found so capable a family at its front. Yet but for the adhesion of Montmorenci and Navarre it is doubtful if the Guises could have carried the majority with them. A yet more important and reliable element in the party was the capital. Paris was a national capital in a sense that could be used of no other town in Europe. It already attracted and re-distributed all the ambition and intellect of France. Italian observers rated its population at 400,000. The French themselves placed the number higher.* In 1546, Marino Cavalli reckons persons connected with the University at from 16,000 to 20,000; those attached to the Parliament and Chambre des Comptes at 40,000. Apart from this it was, he writes, "the Shop of all France." Paris fashions and Paris restaurants already had a European reputation. Paris was, according to Michieli, writing in 1572, the first town in Europe, probably in the world, and Frenchmen did not think life possible if they were prevented from going to Paris. It was their long enforced absence that tempted the Huguenot nobility to the capital in 1572, notwithstanding the notorious danger. "Young widows," writes Tavannes, "made business matters a pretext to rush to Paris to find new husbands, at the risk of their children's health." The Crown and Paris were, in the phrase of La

* These numbers were probably exaggerated. A careful official computation at the outset of the siege reckoned the number of persons to be fed at something over 200,000. The population had, however, by that time undoubtedly decreased. Mendoça reckons the normal population at 550,000, reduced to 400,000 during the siege.

For an interesting account of Paris under the later Valois, see *Eng. Hist. Rev.* 1886.

Noue, the Huguenot captain, the sun and moon of France. The possession of Paris almost implied the possession of Northern and Central France.

There had indeed been discontent in the capital, and the Tuscan envoy believed that an outbreak would have occurred before the war, but that the bourgeois were so rich, and that leaders were lacking. Yet this discontent was probably rather political than religious, and when religion became the dividing line there was no doubt on which side Paris would be found, especially when the Parliament had definitely declared itself against Reform. The Government with difficulty protected the lives of Huguenots against the University students and the lower classes. Intellectually the Parliament and the Sorbonne led the town, and there was no difference of opinion until they split. In the first war the fire at the arsenal, which was attributed to Huguenots, was followed by a massacre of from 800 to 900 heretics. It was enough to say "Voila ung Huguenot," and the person pointed at was hunted down. Then the Parliament interfered and forbade massacre, but hung, strangled, or broke all the rest. "By these means," concludes Claude Haton, "was the city of Paris so well cleared of Huguenots, that the boldest could not have said that there were any." No wonder that La Noue sorrowfully confessed that the novices of the convents and the priests' chambermaids could have swept all Huguenots out of Paris with their brooms.

In the south, as has been seen, Toulouse took the same violent line as Paris, and, generally speaking, the Catholicism of the masses in the large towns was of great service to the party. At Marseilles, at Bordeaux, at Rennes, it required courage to confess the faith amid the cries of "Au feu, au feu, brûle, brûle." Yet it cannot be said that in the early wars the Catholics were often organized, or their full strength utilised. This was mainly due, no doubt, to the non-residence of the higher clergy, and their lack of influence with their flocks.

The Provincial and Municipal governments were, moreover, jealous of independent organizations. Thus at Bordeaux a Catholic syndicate, with a staff of elective officers and a common chest, was formed upon the model of the Huguenot bodies, but was immediately broken up as unconstitutional, the zealous Catholic governor Montluc taking a leading part in its suppression. Nevertheless, an established religion is generally stronger than it seems. It is hard to move, and easy to encroach upon, yet there is always a reaction which gives the force of a new religion. Catholicism had not merely religious, but deep social roots in France. It was connected with all the traditions and the pleasures of the people. Every town had its patron saint; from the King downwards every institution seemed founded on Catholicism. The iconoclasm, the abolition of feast days, the ugly side of Calvinism roused the dormant feeling.* Catholicism had, as well as Reform, its organization, which might easily become political and military, wider indeed, and taking longer to set in motion, yet valuable from the first in civil warfare. The number of clergy, and of laymen professionally dependent on the clergy, was enormous, apart from which every town had its guilds or brotherhoods, under clerical control.

There are, however, only two distinctly-marked movements in the history of the Catholic party previous to the formation of the League of 1585, and these are the massacre of St. Bartholomew, and the Catholic reaction of 1576. It has been argued that the great massacre is not to be ascribed to religious motives; that the Court was prompted by policy, the Parisians by pillage. But the mob was provided and organised by the Catholic municipal authorities; it had always thirsted for the blood of Huguenots; the Government had merely to withdraw the controlling hand. In the other towns

* This accounted for the violent outbreak of Catholicism at Orleans, where the Huguenots had desecrated some fifty churches in and around the towns which originally had much sympathy with Reform.

of France where massacres took place the religious motive was yet more prominent—the attack was led by the high Catholic classes. In many others the well-known Huguenots were saved by being temporarily imprisoned or confined in their houses to keep them safe. Plunder was but an inseparable accessory to all religious strife. The fever heat of St. Bartholomew was followed by a period of stupor. Partly the Catholic party was shocked and morally disorganized by its own crime; partly it could for the moment find no leaders to carry out the movement to its logical consequences. The Crown was forced from political reasons to withhold its hand, and the House of Guise was neither ready nor willing to take the sole responsibility of universal bloodshed. Thus the only immediate result was that many flourishing Huguenot bodies were exterminated, and that Paris was henceforth pledged to revolutionary means. The reaction which made itself felt in the Estates of 1576 bears more immediately on our subject. It was directed almost as much against the Crown as against the Huguenots. It was caused partly by the conditions which the Crown had granted to the heretics at the Peace of Monsieur; but partly by the growing system of favouritism at the Court. The Guises had carefully manipulated the elections, and the Huguenot or Politique population of the south, from fear of the royal mercenaries and Guisard levies, was practically unrepresented. The movement, moreover, was rather revolutionary than constitutional in form, for the assembly of the Estates was merely a convenient vehicle for giving expression to an association which had been organised in entire independence of the Crown, which had rejected the terms granted by or to the Huguenots, and had entered into negotiations with Spain. Leagues of the Catholic nobility had not been uncommon. In 1565 the Association of Guyenne had been formed, in the name of the Provincial Estates, by the governor Montluc and the bishops, and had treated separately with the king of Spain. The

Confrérie du St. Esprit, a secret association, had been founded in Burgundy by Tavannes, and La Sainte Ligue existed in Champagne, of which the Duke of Guise was governor—this latter, it is noticeable, was pledged to the preservation of the Crown for the Valois only so long as they remained Catholic. The League of Picardy of 1576—originally formed to exclude Condé from the stronghold of Peronne—was intended to extend over all Catholic France. Its elective chief was to be obeyed in all and against all; the resolutions of the elective council were to be kept secret. The League was militarily organised, and agents were accredited to foreign Courts to receive and promise assistance, and to the French Court to forward information. The articles of association subordinated the King to the Estates, which should receive all the privileges of the reign of Clovis, or better, if better could be found. All who refused to join were to be treated as enemies; all Catholics to furnish money and arms; to swear never to desert nor disobey it, whosoever might order them to do so. The significance of the movement was that the Catholic nobility pledged itself to revolt from the monarchy if it declined to subscribe to its conditions, and threatened to ally itself with the national enemy. Had not the Crown surrendered, the revolt of the nobles in the War of the Public Weal, and the Huguenot rising of 1563 would again have been repeated. The house of Guise was playing the part previously allotted to the house of Burgundy and the house of Bourbon.

Yet the League did not prosper, and the cause of its failure was the antagonism between the nobles and the people. A similar association was indeed formed in Paris, but the towns were tired of fighting, and distrusted the aristocracy. The Third Estate clamoured at once for the suppression of heresy and the reduction of taxation, and these two objects were incompatible; several provinces refused a subsidy for the war, and when operations began the Picard towns shut their gates against the neighbouring nobles. The only immediate practical effect of the League was that it excluded Condé from the government of Picardy, and so prevented the chances of concerted action between the Huguenot leader and his co-religionists in the Netherlands.

More important, however, was the position which the League was to give to Henry Duke of Guise. He had had, indeed, his full share in St. Bartholomew, but it had hardly brought him to the front. His uncle the Cardinal's death in 1574, left him the most prominent member of his house, and had removed from it the burden of dislike. The family had not been idle, for in 1576 it could control five governments and fifteen bishoprics, while the magistrature, the department of finance, and the municipalities, were full of its creatures. From this moment the Guises never took their eyes from off the Crown. And this ambition directly connects itself with the reaction of 1576.

At the opening of the Estates the papers of one David were produced by the enemies of the Duke. They spoke of the usurpation of the Capets, of the existence of the true descendants of Charlemagne, faithful to the Church, whereas the House of Capet was abandoned to a reprobate sense. The elevation of the Duke of Guise as the head of all leagues would be followed by the annihilation of heresy, and the exclusion of the disobedient Princes of the Blood; the victory would be followed by the seizure of the King, and his confinement in a monastery. Henry of Guise would govern a kingdom consecrated by the abolition of Gallican liberties. These papers were said to have been found in an old box at Lyons upon David's death, but the Catholics professed that they were a Huguenot forgery. Such, however, was not the view of the French minister at Madrid, who had got scent of David's scheme from an independent source.

Of more undoubted authenticity was the genealogical pamphlet of Rosières, a priest of considerable position, who had long enjoyed the intimacy of the Guises. He proved that even Merovius, the successor of Clodio, was an usurper. From the rightful heir sprang Itta, who brought her title to Eustace of Boulogne, a descendant of Charlemagne, whence it descended to the House of Lorraine.*

The constant harping on the female line is to be remarked; the Cardinal of Lorraine had openly confessed his contempt for the Salic Law. Returning to Capetian times the Guises stood before the Valois, and as descendants of the House of Anjou, by the female line, they stood before the Bourbons. Very remarkable is the importance of their marriages, all depending on ultimate rights of succession through females. The Duke of Lorraine married the daughter of Henry II.; Francis of Guise the granddaughter of Louis XII. Henry of Guise wished to marry Margaret, the younger daughter of Henry II.

Mary of Guise had been married to James V. of Scotland, and her daughter to the young king Francis II. Mercœur, a cousin, married the heiress of the Penthièvres, who had claims to the Duchy of Brittany by the female line. Henry of Guise's sister married the Duke of Montpensier, who, as a Catholic, might have supplanted the elder Bourbons, and upon his death she was proposed to the old Cardinal Bourbon, the Catholic Charles X. Mary Stuart was definitively intended for Don Carlos.

Thus it was within the bounds of possibility that the posterity of the Guises should sit on the thrones of France, England, Spain, and Scotland. All this can hardly have been accidental. What is more definite is that the League of Picardy, 1576, substituted in the articles of succession the phrase "à toute la posterité de la maison de Valois" for "maison royale," thus implicitly excluding the Bourbons.

It is yet more remarkable that in 1573, after St. Bartholomew, the Huguenots appear to have contemplated the displace-

* Rosières was imprisoned in the Bastille for this work. He deserved his fate, if only for its dullness.

ment of the Valois by the Guises, not altogether with aversion.*

In 1578 the well-informed Tuscan agent Saracini wrote that the hostility of Henry III. to the Guises had grave reasons; that seeing himself and his brother childless they had set eyes on the succession; hence the King's repressive measures, which the Guises met by courting the favour of the people, and by stimulating rebellion against the Crown.

Since the formation of the League of Picardy the Duke became the unquestioned leader of the Catholic party. Realising the causes of failure, he now took the democratic direction which he was to pursue beyond the limits of revolution. While still keeping touch with the nobility, especially with its younger members, he stimulated and organised discontent in the towns, giving emphasis to the constitutional grievances which found their vent in the Provincial Estates. His activity was marked in Normandy and Brittany, in Burgundy and Champagne, in Guyenne and Dauphiné. The Crown was ere long plied with outspoken deputations, and threatening remonstrances. It was with difficulty that the Estates of Normandy were induced to erase

* "What is to prevent the House of Lorraine, which is known to be descended from Charlemagne, and to have been deprived of the Crown, from recovering it now? It is merely a matter of a clever stroke. For if they care to resort to open force they will put twice as many troops in the field as the King can. They have more friends, and more towns in their favour, than he. For my own part, having seen the little security there is under the present reign, I would much sooner see the Crown in the House of Lorraine than where it is. The Huguenots, permanently disaffected and thoroughly disgusted with the House of Valois, would be very glad, nay more, would lend their aid, to see the House of Lorraine recover what belongs to it, being well assured that it would give them freedom of conscience, and free exercise of religion, and would keep any promise that might have been made, remembering the misfortune that breach of faith has brought upon their master. They have already given the Huguenots some reason to believe that they are not so violent against them, as was said. They have saved many, and secretly save more every day."—*Réveil Matin* of 1573.

the parallel of Rehoboam from their memorial. In this province there was an actual rising. The current complaints turned on the alienation of domain, the constant increase in taxation, and the enforced purchase of salt far beyond the needs or means of the purchaser. There were signs of a yet more revolutionary movement. The Estates of Aunis demanded that the payments due to nobles and clergy should be reduced by one-third. In Dauphiné, as has been seen, Guise stimulated a rising against both King and nobles.

From 1576 to 1584 political discontent was smouldering; it only needed a fresh breath of religious fanaticism to fan it into flame. At this moment the King's brother died. Navarre now became heir-presumptive. It was impossible that the Catholic party should recognise a heretic. Hence arose a very genuine Catholic reaction, and the union of the different political elements of the party; above all, the partnership of the Guises and the capital.

In the winter of 1584-5 was organised in the greatest secrecy the League of Paris, originated by the lawyer Hotman, cousin of the Huguenot publicist, and three popular preachers. The propaganda was conducted through the agency of the various professional and trade corporations. The objects were the suppression of heresy and tyranny; in other words, the exclusion of Navarre, and the expulsion of the King's favourites. It was the work of the ultra-Catholic clergy and laity, alarmed by the prospect of a heretic successor.

In January, 1585, a secret compact for the same objects was formulated by the heads of the House of Guise, the Spanish Commissioners Tassis and Moreo, and the Cardinal of Bourbon. The articles included the exclusion from the Crown of a heretic, or of any who gave indemnity to heretics, the annihilation of heresy, the full acceptance of the Council of Trent. Philip II. offered large subsidies, in consideration of which the Cardinal, who was recognised as heir to the throne, engaged to renounce the Turkish Alliance, to forbid illicit trade with the Indies, to aid Spain in the recovery of Cambrai, now nominally held for the Queen-mother by the adventurer Balagni, to surrender Don Antonio, the *prétendant* for Portugal, and to cede to Spain the inheritance of Henry, Lower Navarre and Béarn, thus giving to the national enemy a foothold to the north of the Pyrenees.

The effect of these parallel movements was to galvanise into fresh life the old League of the Catholic aristocracy. Here, then, in this Catholic reaction are found the three elements of which the original Huguenot party was composed, the princes as represented by the Cardinal of Bourbon, and the Guises, now closely connected with the royal family, the fighting nobility represented by the old League of Picardy, and the bourgeoisie. To the Huguenot ministers may be compared the lower Catholic clergy, both forming as they did a Fourth Estate, and that the most extreme of either party. To complete the parallel, Catherine di Medici, from jealousy of her son's favourites, and dislike of Navarre, is found to give much the same measure of secret support to Henry of Guise as she had originally given to Louis of Condé.*

The League was as much the outcome of political as of religious fermentation, though it was no doubt the religious crisis that brought it to the fighting point. The Cardinal's manifesto might on the political side well be taken for a Huguenot document previous to the opening of the wars. It demanded the reinstatement of the nobility and the Parliaments in all their privileges, the irremovability of all officials by other than judicial means, the appropriation of supplies, and Triennial Estates. Here, then, provision was made for

* Catherine's natural instinct never allowed her to forgive Henry for the unhappy relations with her daughter. She had vainly tried to reconcile the equally guilty pair. Henceforth she is believed to have coveted the succession for the Marquis de Pons, the son of her daughter Claude and the Duke of Lorraine.

the feudal and constitutional interests which the early Huguenots had pressed, while for the republican and federal elements we must look to the attitude of the towns. Just as the Huguenot movement had been from one aspect the revolt of the Bourbons and the Châtillons from the present power of the Guises, so was the League the revolt of the Guises from the future power of the Bourbons. Italian writers regarded the movement as a purely dynastic struggle between these houses, religion being but a flimsy pretext.

The geographical distribution was naturally almost, but not quite reversed. The League extended over the Isle of France, Burgundy, Champagne and Picardy, Normandy and Brittany, and the Central Provinces. The Loire was again the main dividing line, but the League now held the chief towns on the great separatist river and its northern affluents, Orleans, Bourges, and Angers. Southwards the possession of Lyons, the old Huguenot stronghold, thrust a wedge into enemies' territory, while the Catholics controlled also the greater part of Provence, and in Languedoc rested on the southern citadel of Catholicism, Toulouse. The League commanded, according to the calculation of Tavannes, some two-thirds of France No great geographical section was left to royalty. Here and there a town stood firm from jealousy of a Leaguer neighbour. Here and there a governor proved loyal, though rather to the King's favourites than the King. Royalty was forced to choose between League and Huguenot. Intermittent Catholic exaltation and continuous *force majeure* pulled in the same direction. Henry III. was driven to war, and it was fought out at his expense. It was again a three-cornered war, the royal forces and those of the League both acting against Huguenots and Politiques, but quite independently of each other, and, indeed, the Leaguers took towns from royal officers. Naturally enough the extremists won. Henry of Navarre crushed and killed the royal favourite Joyeuse at Coutras, while Henry of Guise broke up the formidable force of German auxiliaries, notwithstanding the terms conceded to them by the King. Peace was the natural result, but peace to the King was more dangerous than war. His action or apparent inactivity had increased his unpopularity; he had neither the courage nor the disloyalty to surrender his favourite, the Duke of Epernon, and Catholic excitement was raised to its pitch by the execution of Mary Stuart, which the King was unjustly suspected of having favoured.

The outcome of discontent was the day of the Barricades, next to St. Bartholomew the most interesting of all days in this rehearsal of the Revolution. The day has at once its political, its dramatic, and its prophetic aspects. It consummated the union between Henry of Guise and the Parisian mob. On the other hand it transports us from the closing scenes of the Valois dynasty to the final tragedy of the Bourbons. Should an historian of the French Revolution transcribe the Tuscan ambassador's report of the Barricades, he might with the majority of readers escape detection. "Guise had sent to Paris over ten thousand men, who, under various pretexts, carried on a propaganda throughout the town, waiting, however, for the Duke's arrival, and watching for a favourable opportunity to secure the King. His Majesty, warned of this large number of strangers who had privily entered Paris, and were secreted in the Leaguers' houses, sent for twelve companies of Swiss, and six of French, to protect him against their plots, and to hunt out these people. Seeing the Swiss posted on guard in the public squares, the Duke suspected that they had entered Paris to thwart him, and perhaps to kill him. He began therefore to arm the populace, and to send his emissaries hither and thither, persuading the townsfolk that the King intended to place a garrison in the town, and take cruel measures against the citizens. Everyone then armed, and barricades were raised across the streets, preventing the Swiss and French companies from advancing. Thus matters stood until midday. The Duke then sent to the Queen-mother, advising her to take steps to allay the disturbance, for on his side he was resolved to die with honour, and if anyone wanted his skin he should sell it very dear. The Queen did what she could—spoke to the King, begged the captains of the quarters to quiet the riot, and get the people to disarm, wrote to some, gave promises to others. She was unable, however, to obtain any result; the riot continually increased, and at last it came to blows between the Swiss and the citizens. Many shots were fired on both sides, and those of the enemy never missed the Swiss, who had no cover, and no practice in street fighting. They were forced to retire from their posts, and give way before the people and the Duke's soldiers, who, covered by the barricades, and firing from windows with great rapidity, and in complete security, despised all the royalists' efforts. Had not the Duke gone in person to allay the tumult, all the Swiss would have been killed. Our people retreating, the enemy gained the *place* which they had evacuated. . . . The King then ordered the Swiss to retire within the palace called the Louvre. The poor King was here practically besieged. So cast down and miserable that he looked the image of death. When night came the troops stood to their arms, while the King bitterly bemoaned his fortunes, bewailing the general treachery. Guise insisted that all the foreign companies cf Royal Guards should be dismissed, and that the King should only retain the ordinary guard. Then he expressed a wish to come to terms, and to present a petition. (Ah! what a petition that was.) Herein everything was contained which tended to his own aggrandisement, and the King's abasement. The poor King, not knowing what to do with himself, not wishing to fall into his enemies' hands, nor even to send for Guise to make his entreaties, as many wished, told his mother to go and find the Duke, and try and quiet the people. While she was gone the King passed out in a coach by a gate near the Louvre, telling his guards to follow. As soon as he was out he raised his head, and shook it, crying, 'God be praised! the yoke is off.'

Then he laughed aloud, and cried, 'Come along, *à la bonne heure.*' Then he sent word to his wife that he was safe and free, and bade her to be calm. Upon hearing this, the cries and the shouts of the ladies rose high as heaven, and they wept for the live King as though he were dead."

Henry, more fortunate than Louis XVI., had no Varennes but his own weak will. Hesitating as yet to join his cousin, he capitulated to the League on its own conditions, which were to be legalised by the Estates-General of Blois. But Guise, and not Henry, was now practically king, and the Duke's assassination may be regarded as an act of tyrannicide, the last resource of the oppressed. Democracy, however, is hundred-headed, and the devoted Gascon guards, who hewed down Guise in the King's Chamber, did as little ·service as the girl who stabbed Marat in the bath.

The Revolution may be said to have opened with the Barricades, but the murder of the Duke of Guise was a yet more critical moment in its history. What the murder of Coligni was to the Huguenots, that was the assassination of its idol to the Catholic party. The lead passed definitely from the nobles and the politicians to the preachers. In the early periods of the war the Huguenots had had the advantage in this respect, there was no Catholic preaching comparable to that of the ministers. But the demand at length produced the supply. The two schools, the scholastic and the grotesque, were fused, the one contributed the trained eloquence of the Catholic revival, the other the ferocity of the Revolution. The Parisian L'Estoile well marks the distinction between the polished eloquence of Panigarola, Bishop of Asti, and the comic gestures and gross indecency of Rose and Boucher. The Jesuits, *esprits choisis,* as they are called by D'Aubigné, provided the most modern intellectual tools. They had too this advantage over the Huguenots, that they preached to the most susceptible congregations of all France, the Catholic masses of the biggest towns. Of all the parochial clergy of Paris, only three were not Leaguers. How influential they were is proved by the fact that among the Forty, which was the supreme military and political Council of the party, there were no less than seven popular preachers, men of no political training whatever. As the Revolution developed, the practice of exacting oaths, and of issuing certificates of orthodoxy, put an additional engine of terrorism into the hands of the clergy. On New-year's day, 1589, Lincestre, Curé of St Barthélemy, after his sermon called upon the congregation to raise their hands and swear to employ their last drop of blood, and the last penny in their purse, to avenge the Guises. To the President de Harlay, who sat in front of him, he twice cried out, "Raise your hand, M. le President, raise it very high; higher still, that the people may see it!" This practice of marking out for popular vengeance suspected members of the congregation became a common artifice with the extreme preachers of the League.

It was through the preachers that, in the towns at least, the Catholic party at last realised its full strength. Not only did they provide the *cadres* of an urban Catholic organization, but the revolutionary exaltation, and the political theory. For dramatic interest it is difficult to surpass the tragedy of Blois, but for the future of the French monarchy the development of the League at Paris had a yet deeper significance. Every revolution will sooner or later search for its philosophical justification, for action cannot permanently be divorced from thought. Hitherto, if we except the fugitive utterances of obscure preachers, any attack upon the Valois dynasty had been directed against deficiency of the genealogical title. Now, however, the very principle of hereditary right was impugned. Kings, it was urged, do not rule by nature or by hereditary right, but by the grace of God, and the visible sign of this is the consecration. The origin, therefore, of the monarchy is religious, and its chief duty religious — the upholding of the Catholic faith. Thus, not the Salic law, as the Parliaments held, but the Holy Union as the League held, was the one fundamental law of the kingdom. Yet it was hardly likely that the attractive and fruitful theory of an original compact should be overlooked by the Catholic publicists, and it became, therefore, necessary to weld together the contractual and the divine elements of monarchy. The people, argued Boucher, make kings, the right of election is superior to inheritance, though a king has been elected the people reserves its power; the people have the right of life and death over kings; the Monarchy is but the result of a mutual contract; in this form it passed from the Merovings to the Carolings, and thence to the Capets. The original contract, it was argued, was framed not merely between king and people, but between God, king, and people; if the king broke his terms with either God or people, the latter was absolved from its allegiance. Here it is easy to trace the religious and the political aspect of the movement. The League, however, did not at once adopt the full conclusions to be drawn from its premises. It at first admitted that hereditary right is not barred by taint of heresy, and thus the nearest Catholic Bourbon, the Cardinal, was accepted. By his death the theory had advanced. Right to the throne consists not in proximity to the old line, but in fervour of Catholicism. Thus one party would take a Guise as being the most Catholic of Frenchmen, another was willing to accept Philip II. as the most Catholic of the world. For what was nationality compared with Catholicism? The Crown becomes elective, the only qualification being orthodoxy.

The logical result of the theory would have been the old Papal view, that all kings held of the Pope as being God's representative, and that of a king's sin the Pope was the sole judge. This indeed had been the earliest form in which the extreme Catholic opposition had manifested itself, for as early as 1561 Jean Tanquerel had written a thesis to prove that it was the Pope's right to depose kings and emperors. But the democracy of the League had little in common with the monarchism of Sixtus V. The Pope had hesitated at first to confirm the League. He might conceivably absolve Henry III.; he might even recognise Navarre. Who therefore is judge? Not Pope, but people. The Pope may absolve from sin, but not from the penalties imposed by the people. The reigning monarch might sit in heaven; but not upon the throne of France. It is then for the people and not the Pope to declare the will of God, for *Vox Populi* is *Vox Dei*. Hence the transition is easy to the theory of the extreme Huguenots, whose arguments and illustrations were borrowed. The kingdom was not hereditary, but elective; the people could elect and the people could depose; the people was above the king. The king and his officers were the ministers of the people; the people was the king, and not the king the people. And who is the people? Not the representatives of the nation assembled at Blois, but the congregations of the faithful at Paris. Urgency required that the Estates should be superseded; the people must rise and rid the country of the King by war or by assassination. It is curious to note how the revolutionist publicists cling to the past while clutching at the future. The old arguments of the Papal-Imperial struggle are again applied—the two swords and the two elements of man. But for Emperor is substituted people, for the Pope frequently the Church, and the Church is regarded not from a monarchical but from a democratic point of view, as being the congregation of the faithful, and thus again the extreme left of Catholicism joins hands with the revolutionary section of the Huguenots.

Such theories were well calculated to stir the masses. Taken up by a more radical section of the nation, and unrestrained by the political views of Calvin, they were carried farther than by the Huguenots. The popular side of the theory soon outgrew the Ultramontane. It threatened a revolution in Church as well as in State. Anti-Leaguers were driven from their benefices, and vacancies in the Parisian churches were filled by popular election, in defiance of the right of patrons. The Bishop of Auxerre was expelled from his diocese. The Pope was threatened and disobeyed. Panigarola refused to retire to his diocese of Asti; Gaetani the legate acted in known opposition to the Papal wishes. Sixtus V. on his death was consigned by the Parisian preachers to the nethermost hell.* Even the more zealous Leaguer bishops found no obedience when they attempted to check the excesses of their flocks.

In its practise the League was no whit less revolutionary than in its theory. Even before the Barricades the lead of the party had passed to a body named the Sixteen, because it was recruited from the sixteen districts of Paris, in each of which was established a revolutionary committee. Thus in its political form the League was a Parisian club, formed by the private influence of private persons. Its members were by no means men of recognised position. They comprised chiefly lower legal officials, tradesmen, and the more violent popular preachers. The party was roughly estimated at some three hundred. The next step was to form corresponding clubs in the other Catholic towns of France. To unite these was soon framed a general council, to which the corresponding clubs sent delegates. But these clubs were in their origin entirely independent of any recognised or constitutional organisation whether royal, provincial, or municipal. The League moreover possessed the most peculiar characteristic of an extreme revolutionary movement. As soon as the club had by prescription obtained a quasi-constitutional position, other clubs are formed inside it containing the more violent elements and they ultimately drive the club, even as the club had

* "God has delivered us from a wicked and politique Pope," preached Aubry. "Had he lived longer, people would have had a fine surprise in Paris in hearing us preach against the Pope, for we should have had to do it."

driven the party. The Confrèrie du Nom de Jésus were the "Mountain" or "the Invincibles" of the League.*

Thus the history of the League is that of the absorption or the abolition of every constitutional organization of France; the municipality, the Estates, the Parliament, the King; what it cannot use it destroys. From the first the League had its army, its chest, even before the Barricades it had its plots to seize the King and his councillors, the Barricades themselves were planned a year before the event. From the first it had the intention of ruling the kingdom through its nominees; when Guise appeared before the people on the day of the Barricades, they cried "à Rheims," the Lorrainer should be the consecrated king of democracy. If the Club could not at once do away with the King, he must be a member of the Club, the Club should utilise what force was left to monarchy.

After the Barricades, the League absorbed the municipality. The municipal constitution, as it had existed since 1380, was overthrown, and a principle of so-called free election re-introduced; members of the lower ranks of the judicature replaced the old municipal families, the League obtained a more or less constitutional position by identifying itself with the municipality of Paris; the town government had in fact fallen from the hands of monarchy into those of the League. It then absorbed the civic militia, replacing the King's officers by its own, occupying the forts of Paris, placing its own governor and garrison in the Bastille. It absorbed also the royal jurisdiction of the Châtelet, one of the oldest and most monarchical institutions of France, the very representation in fact of the monarchy in the capital, dealing with its food supplies and its police. Spreading far beyond Paris, the

---

* So too Orleans had its "Confrèrie du St. Nom de Jésus" in direct opposition to the Bishop and more respectable inhabitants, Leaguers though they were. A similar association at Le Puy ere long exercised a reign of terror over the Catholic upper classes of the Velai. Most Leaguer towns could, in fact, provide a parallel.

strong organization of the League had enabled it to manipulate the Estates General of 1588, to make them practically a committee of the League, which carried the elections, and made the towns adopt its ticket. These Estates, if not of much practical value, are of considerable speculative interest. They contained, as always, a large legal and bureaucratic element, nearly one-half of the Third Estate were lawyers, the rest were chiefly officials. There was the usual lack of genuine, unprofessional, unprejudiced public opinion; the Jack-in-office has ever had an irresistible fascination for the French electorate. The vital question debated by the Estates was, whether they should proceed by resolution or by petition; that is, was the royal legislative prerogative, unquestioned in France, still to exist, or was the Crown merely to ratify and execute the injunctions of the Estates? In home and foreign affairs the King was subordinated to the people's deputies, no peace or war should be made without their consent, no taxes raised, no gifts granted, no Crown influence on elections to be suffered, for the Estates should decide contested elections. The judicature is abased before the legislature. In each sovereign court a permanent Committee of the Estates should receive the complaints of the people, and guard against breaches of their resolutions.

The ecclesiastical and judicial and financial systems, and the royal favourites, were the special objects of attack. It was demanded that pluralism, non-residence, and the holding of benefices by laymen, ladies, and Huguenots, should be abolished. All financial officials should be subjected to a rigid audit, and forced to disgorge ill-gotten gains. Those who had received excessive gifts from the Crown must return two-thirds of the amount. The number of officials, judicial and financial, was stated to be from two thousand to three thousand per cent. above the normal and necessary number, to which they should by both gradual and immediate measures be reduced.

To remove temptation from the Crown in future, the purchase system must be swept away. To remove the excuse for plundering by the troops, and to provide a livelihood for the poorer gentry, it was suggested that the regular cavalry should again be paid by the State. For this purpose the Estates were prepared to grant a *taille*, but they would not trust it to the Crown; it must be raised and expended by a committee of their own.

These demands, however reasonable, threatened the interests of numerous and influential classes. If benefices and Crown gifts were to be taken from the nobles, upon what were they to live? The Crown had already dismissed some six thousand officials, and thus added this number to its enemies. Wholesale reduction of offices was equivalent to repudiation; for, as the Venetian envoys observed, if any one in France had money to invest, an office was the almost invariable investment. The huge fees and gratuities paid for all legal business might indeed be regarded as a tax to meet the interest on the capital invested with the State.

Whatever the Estates might have effected was nullified by the murder of Guise and his brother the Cardinal. The King dismissed the deputies, and the capital again became the centre of revolution. The Sorbonne released the people from its allegiance; the royal arms were torn down; the names of streets which reminded passers-by of the treacherous Valois were changed. Monarchy was provisionally placed in commission.

This naturally led to the abolition or absorption of Parliament, which had, as far as it dared, resisted the League as it had originally resisted the Huguenots.

Bussi le Clercq, once a petty lawyer, now soul of the League and governor of the Bastille, entered the Chamber and arrested several of the most prominent members. The rest followed them out. Others belonging to the two financial courts, the Cour des Aides and the Chambre des Comptes, were arrested in their houses. But Parliament was a useful instrument for judicial tyranny, and therefore the more weak-knee-ed members were restored under the presidency of Brisson. They promised to assist the town of Paris in all things, to contribute to the war, to recognise no treaty except with consent of princes, prelates, towns, and communes. Several members ostentatiously signed the engagement with their blood. Parliament had ceased to be a royal Court; the royal seal was broken, and new seals were made. Of the Provincial Parliaments that of Aix alone voluntarily joined the League. At Toulouse Duranti premier president, and Daffis advocate-general, were murdered; the royal portrait was hung behind Duranti on the gallows, and then suspended in jest from his aquiline nose. Both were zealous Catholics. Duranti had been prominent in the massacre of the Huguenots, and was responsible for the establishment of the Jesuits and Capuchins in his town. They resisted, however, the overthrow of royal authority. Already a separate *mi-partie* chamber existed at Castres. Before long the less revolutionary section of the Parliament of Toulouse was forced from the town and set up a separate court. At no town did the Revolution so rapidly devour its own children. Until the final submission each successive party of violence found itself in turn behind the times.* At Rouen the Parliament which resisted the extremists was broken up and likewise split into two halves. In Brittany a Royalist Parliament continued to sit at Rennes, while a Leaguer Parliament was established at Nantes.

It was at this time also that the executive system of the League, the Council of Sixteen, was generally adopted in the provincial towns, the principle of formation being, however, by class rather than by district. Thus in Toulouse the

* It is characteristic that in the French Revolution the two towns which chiefly distinguished themselves by indigenous massacre were Paris and Toulouse, the scenes of the Red Terror, and the White. It is hard to decide which of the two was the more constant to the principles adopted in 1589.

Parliament was forced to assent to the surrender of all municipal authority to the Eighteen; at Le Puy all powers civil and military were committed to the Twenty Four; the pettiest League town had its Twelve or Six. It was a golden age for the professional politician of the lowest class, and frequently the gentry, however Catholic, as in the Velai, had to suffer dearly for their resistance to the wildfire of revolution. Southern Catholic France was as definitely withdrawn from all contact with monarchy as had previously been the Huguenot and Politique section of Languedoc. The Catholic Estates of Languedoc elected its governor from the house of Joyeuse, raised its taxes, levied war upon Damville, and contracted its alliance with neighbouring Leaguer governors. The Provincial Estates were the one ancient institution which seemed destined to be strengthened by the struggle. On the plea of urgency, the revolutionists of Paris had set aside the sovereignty of the Estates General, which had hitherto headed the programme of the party. The real ruling body of Catholic France was now the Council of Forty, at the head of which stood the Duke of Mayenne as lieutenant-general. It claimed all the prerogatives of the Crown, the right of pardon, the receipt of royal revenues, the appointment to all State offices and Crown benefices. It made a bid for popularity by lessening the burden of taxation, and abolishing purchase in the judicature. Immediate necessities were supplied by Spanish subsidies, and by the organised ransack of the houses of suspected royalists. Yet the revolution had reached its zenith, it contained the germs of destruction within itself. To outward appearance indeed the murder of the King was the culminating triumph. Paris went wild with joy. Mme. de Montpensier and her mother, Mme. de Nemours, harangued the people from the steps of the Cordeliers, and hung green scarves, "the livery of idiots," round the necks of rejoicing citizens. The assassin Clément became a St. Thomas of Canterbury to revolutionary France. No shrine was so frequented as his tomb. Those who were drowned in returning from the pilgrimage were also martyrs. To die for the faith delivered the soul from purgatory, until it was realized that it delivered the pockets of the living from providing masses. France had now a king of its own election—Charles X., the Cardinal of Bourbon. Navarre was in full retreat from the neighbourhood of Paris.

Yet the League had a dangerous enemy in its own lieutenant-general. The fighting element could not permanently have sympathy with the semi-clerical, semi-democratic element. As long as Henry III. had lived the two sides were tolerably united, their common aim was negative—the King's suppression. But the positive question, that of the succession, was soon to divide them, for the elected King was a prisoner, and in the course of 1590 died.

The death of Henry of Guise had seemed to bring his family nearer to the throne; yet to the fortunes of the Revolution his loss was irreparable. He alone could lead both nobles and people, he alone dared utilise the strength of numbers. The King's violent act had perhaps saved the monarchy, though at the expense of his own life. It was a misfortune that the Duke's son was a prisoner in Henry's hands. His successor, Mayenne, was not the character to lead a Revolution, for he saw obstacles too clearly. Duke Henry had been a born demagogue, rapid in conception and action, yet patient and prudent; his combination of sweetness and strength won alike the soldier and the populace. Free from all scruple, he delighted in an atmosphere of trouble. Mayenne was no demagogue; he had many of the feelings of the noble class, and disliked the Sixteen and its democracy. He was a sound but indolent soldier, and a cautious politician; too cautious, perhaps too honest, for his place. The Parisians never wearied of satirising the free-living general, who could make war only upon his border, and who hampered his military movements by a harem. A warrior indeed who, on falling from his horse, required four soldiers to replace him, was no match for Navarre, who would not spare the time to undress or wash.

There was as yet no open conflict between Mayenne and the Parisians, but each side became conscious of coming strife. For Mayenne were the statesmen, the Leaguer nobility, the higher judicial and municipal families. Against him were the Sixteen, the clergy, the friars, the mob, and above all the King of Spain, represented by Mendoça, and later by Ybarra, who became the almost *ex officio* leaders of the ultra-democratic party.

Mayenne took the offensive. He had already modified the Council by introducing an aristocratic and Parliamentary element. He now practically abolished it by establishing a Privy Council, attached to his person. The Forty, he urged, represented a form of republic neither customary nor good in a kingdom. The name of the Council was henceforth omitted in all documents. The Council was the factor in the unconstitutional Constitution which made the Revolution national as well as Parisian; for it was attended by the provincial delegates, and could speak in the name of France. Its abolition was the end of federalism; each town had now to provide for its own defence, and the war would be decided by the soldiers. The questions of the future were rather religious and personal than constitutional.

Yet the Revolution had its hour of reaction. The siege of Paris resulting from the battle of Ivri again made the capital the centre of all France, and in Paris the extreme no-surrender party came to the front, led by the Duchess of Montpensier, the Spanish Ambassador, and the Papal Legate Gaetani. Paris endured a famine, to which that of 1570 was child's play. For some time rations of bread, with a piece of cat or dog, were served to the poor; but cats, dogs, rats, and mice rapidly disappeared. The hide of every beast in Paris was devoured. Candle grease became a luxury. The Duchess of Montpensier advised the people to dig up bones from the cemeteries and grind them into flour, but death was found to result from the Duchess of Montpensier's bread. Mme. de

Montpensier was asked for her pet dog to feed the poor. She replied that she was keeping it for her last meal. Noble ladies declared that they would eat their children rather than admit the heretic, and the more suffering classes took them at their word. The German mercenaries chased the children down the streets, as the children had chased the dogs. Everything, sarcastically wrote L'Estoile, was ruinous except sermons, of which starving people could have their bellyful. The defence indeed was organised rather from the pulpit than the barrack. The clergy denounced the Politiques day by day, and this marked them out for murder. The Legate received a regiment of thirteen hundred priests and monks, all marching, with arms on their shoulders, and their frocks tucked up. The Scotch curé Hamilton acted as sergeant-major, halting them at intervals to sing a psalm and fire a volley. Yet they had to admit the growing discontent; one of the curés declared that if the members of his congregation were vivisected, a big Bearnois would be found in every heart. Armed mobs clamoured for bread or peace (Pain ou Paix). Blank walls were scrawled with charcoal pasquinades against the Sixteen and the Spaniards.

The Duke of Parma with his Spanish troops arrived only just in time to save the town. With his arrival the Sixteen regained their spirits and their power, they demanded from Mayenne the restoration of the Council General, the sole and sovereign body of the party, thus implicitly renouncing the sovereignty of the Estates General. They claimed that an extraordinary tribunal should practically supersede Parliament. They forced him to admit a Spanish and Neapolitan garrison.*

* These troops were lodged in the deserted colleges, and their horses stabled in the chapels. The Revolution was a permanent blow to the University of Paris. It may be called the dividing line between the old and the new system. Out of forty colleges only one continued in residence. Some were occupied by peasants from the environs, the quadrangles of others became choked with briar and bramble. (*Cf.* Pattison's *Casaubon*, 2nd ed., p. 159.)

They now called upon him to purge the Parliament, to restore to Paris the Grand Council and the seal, to destroy all castles and forts round the Capital. The reign of terror began. The curé Pelletier preached that no justice could be expected from Parliament, it was time to play the knife. "A dose of Politique blood" had long been the specific recommended by his party. Boucher's sermons were full of "blood and butchery." He cried that they must kill all Politiques, that with his own hands he would strangle the dog of a Béarnois. The death of Politiques is the life of Catholics, preached Commolet. "Another bleeding of St. Bartholomew," shrieked Rose, "and cut the throat of our disease."

A secret committee of ten was appointed to act as the executive of the extremists. In each quarter there was a "red list" of the future victims. Opposite each name was written C for Chassé, D for dagué, or P for pendu.* There was to be a St. Bartholomew for the Politiques. The Parliament was naturally struck first; even during the siege the Sixteen would have made short work with them but for the governor Nemours. Now the first president Brisson and two others were strangled, and their bodies exposed upon the gibbet. For this Paris was not ripe; the Spanish and Neapolitan garrisons refused to carry out the proscription. The Neapolitan Colonel, when asked for aid, said that he wished all heretics in the Inquisition, all traitors in the Seine, and significantly added, all scoundrels on the gallows. De Maistre was invited to return to Parliament. He replied that he would only come to get the murderers hung. La Rue, one of the foremost and least reputable of the Sixteen, left the party, protesting against its cruelty. The populace, far from being stimulated by the crime, looked with stupefied horror on the hanging bodies. The Archbishop Gondi thought it prudent to leave the town. Even Mme. de Montpensier broke away from the Terrorists, and summoned Mayenne to

* Our authority, L'Estoile, saw his own name marked D.

Paris. Mayenne entered the town, and forced Bussi to surrender the Bastille. Four leaders of the Sixteen were hung without trial, and its council forbidden to meet. All secret clubs were prohibited. Parliament was re-organized, the upper bourgeoisie armed against any possible reaction, and even negotiated with the King. Mayenne treated the clergy roughly, told them not to dabble in politics, but to confine themselves to their theology; "he knew," it was reported, how to destroy "leur petit empire de Sorbonne." In vain the preachers strove to flog the party into life. Divisions arose even among themselves. Panigarola had denounced the bloodthirsty vindictiveness of the French, directed even against the dead. Rose, the most violent and grotesque, showed signs of compromise. In the Estates of 1593 the party of the Sixteen hardly survived except among the clergy; in the Third Estate, out of twelve Parisian deputies eight were Politiques. The League still existed as a Catholic union for the election of a Catholic Prince, but the revolution was over, the dynastic question alone remained.

There was indeed no lack of constitutional grievances. The cause of financial reform, originally championed by the Estates of Orleans and Pontoise, was now taken up by provincial Catholic Estates, and were re-echoed in the *cahiers*, or instructions given to their deputies by the Leaguer towns. The Estates of Burgundy refused to increase the tax on salt, or to find any fresh supplies even for the payment of their own representatives. They would grant no taxes beyond those which had been levied thirty years ago. When Tavannes, the son of the old marshal, represented that they were exposing themselves to certain invasion, they replied that they would meet the enemy at home, but would incur no fresh charges. Many deputies in the Estates General declined a proposal for a fresh subsidy for the purpose of raising lanzknechts. The deputies of Rouen were instructed to repeat the complaint, well-worn even in the reign of Louis XI., of the oppression of the regular soldiery. They called for due protection for the peasants and their crops. Their Parliament was indeed to be purged of heretics; but, on the other hand, all supernumerary offices must be extinguished, and the purchase of judicial and financial offices abolished. They protested that no additional *tailles* or subsidies should be raised without the consent of the provincial Estates of Normandy. So too the town of Rheims demanded that the excesses of the gendarmerie should be suppressed, and that the old national infantry force, the legionaries, an experiment of Francis I., should be re-organised; that the taxes should be reduced to the standard of Louis XII. Yet more radical were the views of the Third Estate at Troyes. It suggests a scheme for a representative executive; the elected king should have an elective council, consisting of Catholic princes and great officials, checked by a standing committee of three deputies from each Estate in every Province, to be elected every three years in the several Provincial Estates. To these latter belongs in the last resort the sovereignty of France, for no *tailles* should be raised but by their consent. The town of Amiens would deprive the King of his legislative authority, which as yet had scarcely been questioned, except by the Judicature, for the future no edict should be issued without consent of the Estates. There are signs too of the old alliance between the clergy and the Third Estate. The clergy of Auxerre complain indeed of the unconstitutional taxation of their order; but they also demand the suppression of judicial offices created in recent reigns, and the reduction of general taxation to its normal limits. In all quarters is to be traced the jealousy of the Third Estate for the nobles, the captains, and the governors. It is demanded that all fortresses and chateaux not absolutely necessary for national defence should be demolished; that the gentry should be forbidden to keep garrisons; that governors should have no right of levying money, supplies, or forced labour; and that they should cease from interference in matters of justice and finance.

The people of Catholic France realised that the election of a new dynasty gave an opportunity for imposing capitulations which might have reduced the power of the monarchy to the level of that of Poland. But unfortunately for the prospects of Reform, the question of the election itself was so absorbing that all other demands passed out of sight. The Revolution and the Monarchy were really incompatible, and France was not as yet prepared altogether to forego the latter. The continuance of opposition to Navarre was impossible without Spanish subsidies, and these Philip was not disposed to grant unless his own claims or that of his daughter were recognized. The Extremists were indeed prepared to meet his views. The Sorbonne declared that the country must be saved from heresy whether by preserving or dividing the monarchy. The old party of the Sixteen was ready to hand over the kingdom to Philip, who should no longer be styled King of Spain, but "le grand Roi"; the decrees of Trent should be recognized; the Spanish Inquisition introduced; Philip would anticipate Louis XIV. in levelling the Pyrenees; a Spanish king should rule a republican France, with its quadrennial Estates, its free judicature, and its reduced imposts; Paris should be but the French Madrid. But the nation at large refused to surrender its nationality to its religion. The Leaguer towns almost unanimously clamoured for a French Catholic king. The anti-national character of the extremists was at length fully realised. The unceasing satire of the Huguenots and Politiques on Spanish doubloons had at last struck home. The scrawl which was always reappearing on the blank walls of Paris became the motto of all France—"Pereat Societas Judaica cum tota gente Ibera." The wars were to end as they began, with the cry against the foreigner. The Spaniard succeeded the Italian and the Lorrainer.

But where should a French king be found? Candidates seemed to spring only from the hybrid houses of the Borderland. The Duke of Savoy and his relative, the Duke of

Nemours, relied on their connection with Francis I.* From the House of Lorraine five candidates at least were in the field—the Duke of Lorraine, the Duke of Guise, Mayenne, his son, and Mercœur. The House was divided against itself. Its head had struck the first note of discord when he had discouraged the League at its outset. It became evident that the Lorrainers had no genuine love for France, that every member was playing for his own hand. Mercœur, the most consistent and the most resourceful, was neglected and discouraged by his house, and yet he alone succeeded in kindling the enthusiasm of the lower rural classes. His resistance in Brittany was the most creditable feature in Leaguer military records, it went far to close the century of union between Brittany and France.

The League in its extreme form had proved the solvent of the Catholic party, and Mayenne had been the solvent of the League. The real force of the great revival rested on the union of Paris and the capable house of Lorraine, on the combination of the revolutionary religious with the personal political element. Mayenne had divided his own house, and broken up this union; he had reduced Catholic France to a system of communal defence. Town after town fell away to royalty; it is doubtful whether the majority in the towns had ever been really Leaguer any more than they had been Huguenot. Religious enthusiasm had for a moment welded together political elements whose antagonism had hitherto hampered religious or constitutional reform. But the closer the temporary union the wider was the ultimate breach. The nobility was fast breaking from the Revolution. Its patriotism revolted against Spanish domination, its interests were irreconcilable with

* If the Duke of Savoy could not gain the monarchy, he was dangerous enough to aid in its dismemberment. He was formally recognized in Provence as Count. Had he retained his hold Provence would have fallen away from France, and been nominally re-united to the Empire. He had already wrested from France Saluzzo, the last of her Italian possessions.

those of the Third Estate. In the Estates of 1593 only two possible noble candidates could be found in all Paris and its viscounty. From other districts only a single noble representative appeared. There is abundant evidence of the fear among the nobles of a yet lower depth of democracy than had yet been sounded.

As the League resembled the Huguenot revolt in the political elements out of which it was composed, and in the political theory which it ultimately formulated, so was it also reproducing some of its more extreme provincial manifestations. There was a tendency both towards communal disintegration and towards a social rising of the lowest classes. There were fears that these two tendencies, the one urban and the other rural, might combine, as had been the case in the days of the Jacquerie, and as had been threatened in the German peasants' revolt of 1525. Peasant revolts actually occurred. Under the priests of the League, the peasants rose against the nobles in Normandy. "We went in," writes Tavannes, "and burnt their villages; but where a hundred were acting a thousand were looking for the result." With the slightest success the flame would have run over the whole of France. But the peasants lacked leaders. The House of Guise alone dared rely upon the rural democracy. Henry of Guise had encouraged the Calvinist peasantry of Dauphiné; his cousin Mercœur, in Brittany, led the lower classes against the Catholic but royal nobility.

"Their idea," states Tavannes, "was to live after the manner of the Swiss—to be exempt from taxation, to pay no rents, and perform no services for their lords." Land for nothing, and another class to pay the taxes, is the invariable programme of rural revolution. The Swiss confederation had often nearly split upon the dualism between town and country, the French Revolution was in its early days endangered by the traditional feuds, and the same difficulty of combination existed now. But, above all, the French peasantry lacked the practice of arms. The reasons which had prevented the French from forming a national infantry was a safeguard against revolution. The German peasants, with their strong lanzknecht element, had been far more dangerous.

It had been all along the weakness of the Catholic party that it could not utilize its numerical strength. The League indeed had brought the lower urban classes into the struggle. Tavannes believes that it failed because it dared not arm the peasants; he would have armed them with pikes on the Swiss model. They would have exterminated Huguenotism, and with it the nobility of France.

The *noblesse de robe* had been threatened by the Estates General, persecuted by the mobocracy; their importance was lost, whether in war or in revolution. Their sympathies had always been with the Crown; their patriotism took the form of Constitutionalism; the Salic law, they urged, was the one fundamental law of the country. Their example was followed by the diplomatists who found no sure footing in a democracy, who were the natural rivals of the Spanish *corps diplomatique*, and by the upper bourgeoisie, who had been deprived of the command of the municipalities, and whose trade was ruined. A large proportion of the Episcopate had early rallied round the throne. The League had been founded by the parochial clergy, forwarded by the friars. The tendency of the former was towards democratic Gallicanism, towards popular election of the clergy, that of the latter towards democratic Ultramontanism. Both were destructive of the Episcopate, which had been treated as non-existent. Once again it was proved that in France the Church could not divorce itself from the Crown; the hierarchy had been threatened as much by the Leaguer curés as by Huguenot ministers.

The position of the League became ridiculous; its political life was closed. Yet its religious vitality was still strong, and at this moment, just as the political question had divided the party of the League, the religious question was threatening the unity of the Bourbons. The Cardinal of Vendôme and his brother the Count of Soissons were forming a third party, cleaving to the inalienable right of the Bourbons, but following the dictates of the nation in insisting on a Catholic branch of the house.

Navarre grasped both the opportunity and the danger. His conversion could not now be attributed to fear of Guise or Spaniard. He recognised the Estates as uttering the deliberate sense of the majority. To delay was dangerous. The Estates of 1593 did little else, but they forced Henry to renounce his creed.

The King's conversion and absolution unloosed the tongues, and untied the hands, of the Politiques of Paris. The risk was great, for the revolutionists still controlled the municipality, and the foreign troops were still quartered in the capital. It was with fear and trembling that the first white scarves showed themselves in the shivering dawn, but their numbers gradually swelled, and with the admission of Henry at the Porte Neuve the long-brooding danger of a St. Bartholemow for the Politiques was at an end.

The mass gave Henry Paris, and Paris gave Henry France. Again to quote Tavannes: "The capture of Paris or the King is half the victory in civil war." The King had taken Paris, and Catholicism had captured the King. With which lay the victory?

The failure of the League implied the defeat of democracy, and of the greatest of the princely houses, in which the Crown had long found its antagonists. But for Catholicism it was a gain; for the League already contained the disruptive forces which were ultimately to break up the Church of France. To a system of authority the popular preacher of the sixteenth century was as dangerous as the *philosophe* of the eighteenth; indeed in the revolution of the future the successors of the preacher of the League and of the Huguenot minister were to reappear, shoulder to shoulder.

Neither ultramontane Leaguers nor Huguenots had now triumphed, but the national Catholics. They insisted on a Catholic king, and the King must needs be Catholic. They obtained the universal restoration of the mass, and of the Church property. They secured the exclusion of Huguenot worship from the districts where Catholicism was most zealous. Catholicism was henceforth without dispute the national religion. In the religious conflict the more conservative element had won.

III.

THE CROWN

THE humiliating position of the Crown throughout the Wars of Religion was as much the result of misfortune as of fault. It was à necessity of nature that the lustre of monarchy should be temporarily obscured. The Capetian dynasty had been founded on foreign war, and developed by foreign war. It was the symbol of French unity against the foreigner. The advent of peace had always been a danger-signal. The natural turbulence of the French nobility, which had found its vent in war, whether defensive or offensive, was turned into less patriotic channels. War had brought the nobles out of their feudal isolation, and gathered them closely round the Crown, but this was not all gain. Being so near the Crown they must needs control it for personal or class interests, and were this impossible they would fall back on their previous independence. It was likely that under any circumstances the close of the Spanish wars would have been followed by the same internal troubles which at the close of the English wars had strained all the resources of the governments of Charles VII., Louis XI., and the Regency of Anne of Beaujeu. The Constable Bourbon, the greatest nobleman in France, deserting in time of war, had found no following, notwithstanding the existence of general discontent. It was certain that in time of peace every malcontent grandee would beckon to any foreign power that had access to his province.

The difficulties of the Crown were increased tenfold by the introduction of the religious factor. Hitherto the bureaucracy and the middle classes had on the whole stood by the monarchy in its conflict with the nobles. Now, however, they failed to recognise the factious element in the great party leaders, it saw in them only the champions of their own religion, whether Catholic or Reformed. Religion, moreover, was becoming more than nationality. The Chancellor L'Hôpital opened his speech to the Estates General of Orleans by saying that there was now more love between an Englishman and Frenchman of the same religion, than between two Frenchmen of different forms of faith. The Huguenots brought the English to Havre, and promised Calais; they deluged France with reiters and lanzknechts; they agreed to surrender to the Palatinate the one great conquest of Henry's reign, the Three Bishoprics, the military keys of Lorraine. The Catholic grandees from the first intrigued with Spain, and ended by well-nigh dismembering France. The monarchy could not hold the nation together when religion was set against religion. The more genuine eager minds, without being intentionally disloyal, turned to their party chiefs, to Guise or Coligni. Coligni once said that he could raise a better army in four days than the King in four months. The same was certainly true of the Duke of Guise. The Crown was left face to face with two parties, each stronger than itself.

But if the principle of monarchy was for the moment weak, its *personnel* was weaker when the storm burst upon it. "What," replied Henry IV. to a critic of Catherine di Medici, "could a poor woman have done with her husband dead and five small children upon her hands, and two families who were scheming to seize the throne, our own and the Guises. . . . I am astonished that she did not do even worse." Catherine's chief adversary has been among Frenchmen, her most generous apologist. The French of all ages seem to have a singular antipathy to the Italian character, and Catherine was eminently Italian. Her evil reputation has been due to French sources; she has been the scapegoat for the sins of the French nation. Both creeds and all classes disgraced themselves, and the shame of all was cast upon the foreigner, who perhaps of all most consistently strove to guard the interests of France. No treason can be imputed to the Italian as to Coligni or to Guise. Catherine's name is vulgarly associated with shameless immorality and wholesale poisoning. The libels of Huguenot pamphleteers and Guisard popular preachers have been handed down through generations, and yet they were hardly intended to be believed. There is every reason to think that she was entirely faithful as wife and widow to a husband who did not deserve her affection. If it be true that after the death of Eléonore de Roye she wished to marry Condé, it was a wish innocently shared by many other ladies. There is not the slightest evidence for attributing to her a single case of poisoning. In the sixteenth century everyone lived too freely. Sanitation was neither natural nor scientific. To die of natural causes was unfashionable, a sign of unimportance, and consequently, in the upper ten thousand, every death that was not of violence, was liable to be ascribed to poison. Yet Catherine perhaps deserves to suffer for her one great crime, the massacre of St. Bartholomew, and the cruelties which completed it.

Catherine was not attractive. Frenchmen regarding the marriage as a *mésalliance* thought her vulgar. Her prominent eyes, and projecting lips recalled her great uncle, Pope Leo X. She was not tall, but largely made, and grew unduly stout. To correct this tendency, she took constant exercise on foot, tiring out all her suite. "Constant movement," wrote Lippomano, "gives her a good appetite, and if she takes exercise enough for two, she eats in proportion." Hence she suffered much from indigestion, and as time went on from gout. At her meals she loved incessant chatter, and was an immoderate laugher, enjoying especially the libels on herself. Genuinely good-natured, she never sought out nor punished the authors of the scandalous pamphlets; her one continued feeling of vindictiveness was against Montgomery, who had accidentally killed her husband, and afterwards flaunted the broken spear upon his scutcheon. Lavish alike in gifts and alms she had no faculty of saying no. If she could not content an applicant with substantial grants, she would dismiss him laden with promises. As a girl she had been well educated, and had literary tastes; but her troubled life gave no scope for study, though she retained to the end the passion of her family for building and art collections. Her naturally joyous and easy nature could alone have supported her through the great trials of her life. She was never known but once, states Lippomano, to be really angry. On the other hand, she was tortured by jealousy, a natural result of her early married life, and of her being shelved both under her husband and her eldest son. She had a craving to be important, to have a hand in all state business, she loved to hear all good results ascribed to herself, all evil consequences to bad advisers. Her efforts indeed were vain, for, in Correr's words, " If anything is refused it is put down to her; if there are failures, to her they are ascribed."

Notwithstanding her love of flattery she trusted no one, and rightly, for she had been much deceived. She placed more reliance in her Italian followers than in the French, and this added to her unpopularity. Her religion was of the formal Medicean type, with a strong taint of superstition, of belief in amulets and prophecies, an almost universal feature of the Court. She respected the established, and despised enthusiasm; she could not understand the real force of the religious motive, thinking that questions could be settled by diplomacy and compromise, believing with Machiavelli that religion should be utilised as an engine of Government, using, in the phrase of Tavannes, the Huguenots as men use leeches to draw bad blood. Thus her usual policy consisted in Edicts of Pacification, followed by small continuous encroachments. She told Alva that the results had been very good; and Henry III. pursued the same method with success, making orthodoxy the qualification for Court favour. It was, after all, the policy of Richelieu, and the earlier period of Louis XIV. The financial factor in the Huguenotism of the upper classes was worth reckoning with.

While not personally vicious Catherine had not a high moral standard. Passionately fond of her children, she spoilt them by indulgence. The ladies of her Court bore no good reputation, and she was believed to utilise their charms for political ends. Frenchmen ascribed the vices of the age to her instruction, but the Italian could now teach them nothing that they did not know too well. The French Court under her *régime* was certainly no worse than under her predecessors, and her loss of influence was marked by a far lower pitch of degradation.

Catherine's abilities are somewhat hard to gauge. Frenchmen probably overrated them for evil, and Italians for good. Of her industry there can be no doubt. No French monarch has worked harder for his country, and none perhaps, except Louis XI., has personally visited so much of France. She thought lightly of a journey from Paris to Nérac, and with every piece of work and every journey grew younger and more jovial. But industry is not ability. Among the numerous critics of Catherine's faculties the Venetians are probably the least prejudiced. "An intellect acute and genuinely Florentine," wrote Barbaro early in her career; "a clear and intelligent business woman." "Perhaps too conceited," adds Correr, "and I do not say that she is a Sybil, but there is no prince who would not have lost his head amid these troubles, much more a woman and a foreigner without trusty friends, constitutionally timid, never hearing the truth. Nevertheless all the respect that is still given to monarchy is due to her."

These views are in substantial agreement with that of Henry IV., who ascribed it to her prudence and her cunning that the schemes of both great houses were defeated, and that her three sons reigned in turn. That France needed a masculine genius, and not a business woman, was no fault of Catherine's.

The Queen's personal political failures were due in part to the hereditary policy of a weak but absolute Italian power. She disliked at once the great princely houses which temporarily overshadowed the Crown, and the permanent constitutional checks. The part that Clement VII. had played between France and Spain, Catherine revived as between Guise and Bourbon. She hoped to balance one against the other, wishing to support the weaker, yet not daring; forced to follow the stronger, and consequently getting no thanks. As to Clement were attributed the two great tragedies of Italy—the sack of Rome, and the fall of Florence; so to Catherine were ascribed the two great tragedies of France—the Massacre of St. Bartholomew, and the murder of Henry of Guise. The latter accusation was indirectly true. She had overrated her influence with her son, and this proved fatal to her friends. She believed that Henry would do nothing without her advice, but, as Tavannes remarks, "Un sage entrepreneur ne se fie en sa mère propre." For years indeed she had struggled against the conviction that the darling of all her children had broken from her leading-strings; and indeed Henry's indolence and frivolity left her a large residuum of power. From his accession until the Barricades she had reconciled all the party chiefs in turn. She had even reconciled Henry and his brother, her daughter Margaret and Navarre. But for her, wrote the Tuscan envoy more than once, the Seine would long ago have run with blood. She wrongly believed that she could reconcile the King and his tyrant.

Characteristically enough her passion for compromise, her physical energy, and her kindly heart, together caused her death.

The tale is best told in the Tuscan agent Cavriana's letter of January 6th, 1589. He writes that, on the preceding day the Queen was taken to a better life owing to a pleurisy which passed into another malady called peri-pneumonia, which meant inflammation of the lungs, and ended in apoplexy, "She caught the disease by exposing herself to a chill on New-year's day, which was extremely cold and blusterous, against the doctor's advice, and after having wept copiously over the harsh words which the Cardinal Bourbon addressed to her when at the King's request she went to see him and announce his liberation. 'Madame,' he said, 'if you had not deceived us, and lured us here with fair words, and under a thousand guarantees, the two would not be dead, and I should be at liberty.' She was so wounded by these words that she returned to her room and had a relapse of the complaint of which she was hardly quit, much less thoroughly cured." Here the worthy Tuscan quite broke down. "Pray pardon me. I can write no more for grief, and for the tears that keep a-flowing when I call to mind the merits of that great Queen, my own kind mistress, and if you should not find my letter all that it ought to be, pray take my passionate sorrow for excuse. Another day I will give better satisfaction." "With her," in another line he cries, "is dead all that kept us in life." Better women and more glorious queens have had less touching epitaphs.

Of Catherine's three royal sons, the only self-subsistent figure is Henry III., at once pathetic and contemptible. By nature gifted with taste and talent, he was cursed by hereditary disease and a predisposition to premature vice. Zealously Catholic, even to his disadvantage, naturally chivalrous and honest, all his good qualities were nullified by lack of will. He was everything by turns and nothing long. It is hard to believe that the abnormal effeminacy, the hanging earrings, the frizzed head, the puppy dogs, the girl-like admiration for his favourites, were not the result of constitutional ill-health. Yet he had fought at Jarnac and Moncontour, and he never faltered when Guise had to be struck down. When Clement stabbed him he tore the dagger from the wound and plunged it in the assassin's jaw. No one realized more clearly that he was unfit to be a king. Retirement and pleasant society[*] were his ideal. Yet, when forced to business, he showed intelligence. Twice he thwarted the Estates General of France, twice he out-manœuvred Guise. Under the most humiliating circumstances he showed a readiness and a dignity which recovered his position. His contemporaries dwelt with curiosity upon this embodiment of contrasts. Temperate in eating and drinking, he was immoderate in all else—in vice, in dancing, in penitential exercises. The lavish expenditure on his pleasures was aggravated by the equally expensive craze for introducing and endowing ascetic religious orders. His misfortunes were his fault; yet it is hard not to pity the least creditable of French kings, with his genuine agonies of remorse, and the constitutional impossibility of a better life. Estranged by his own act from his mother, hating his brother almost from birth, trusting not even his own favourites, he sat alone towards his end, day after day, constantly working and writing, striving to save his throne when it was too late; with his hair and beard turned white, and his teeth gone, though he was barely thirty-six. The energy and skill with which he lured Guise to his fate, the imperturbability with which he announced his crime, his expressed resolve to be a king at last, all betokened a re-awakening of the will. Had he followed up his blow, half France would have applauded. But he relapsed into listless change of purpose, and within a week his well-wishers realized that he was lost, and foretold his coming murder. Such were the persons on whom it devolved to pilot the monarchy through the Scylla and Charybdis of confront-

[*] "The position of a private gentleman," writes Tavannes, "with an income of £10,000, was Henry's idea of happiness."

ing religions. It remains to consider what possibilities of action lay before them.

There were four alternatives which the Crown might take in relation to the religious struggle, and which from time to time it actually adopted. Of these the first two may be called professional, the latter unprofessional. The king might act purely as judge and mediator, make terms between the two religions and enforce them. Or he might act as military leader of the nation, turn thoughts away from religious strife back to national glory, and unite Catholics and Huguenots against the foreigner.

On the other hand, the Crown might become a faction leader, and either gain command of the most dangerous party, and thus neutralize the danger to itself, or by joining the weaker establish a balance between the two. Finally it might adopt a perversion of the first alternative, and raise a third party to a position of equal independence with the other two. The history of the Crown throughout the Religious Wars consists in the ringing of the changes on these alternatives. The first was the view of L'Hôpital, the second that of Coligni. The Crown itself unfortunately was driven or disposed to adopt the latter two, though not without many genuine impulses towards a more professional policy. Before the outbreak of civil war, L'Hôpital stated in the assembly of St. Germain, that it was odious and absurd to advise the King to put himself at the head of one party, and to exterminate the other, and this view he never ceased to urge upon the Queen-mother. Catherine seems honestly to have adopted it. It was no fault of hers that the Edict of January, the basis of all future arrangements, was not preserved. After the Peace of Amboise, she reverted to the Chancellor's policy. She sent the most moderate royalists into the provinces to enforce the terms of pacification. She took the young King on a progress throughout France, and seems to have struggled to attain to the judicial conception of the monarchy. But the Crown required both a judicial staff to give expression to its wishes, and an executive to enforce them. For the former task the Parliaments were most unfitted. Seated in the heart of the great Catholic cities, or in the ring of frontier provinces, they were subject to local passions, and had not the unity which might enable them to adopt a professional standpoint. When religious troubles came upon England, the judicature also fell into disrepute, but the cause of this was its subservience to the monarchy. In France its failure was due first to its insubordination, and finally to its weakness. In the religious crisis, the pride of France, the great judicial institution for which she paid so dearly, lost its credit. No Huguenot could hope for justice in the ordinary tribunals, and hence the constant demand for *mi-partie* chambers in which each religion should be represented. Political abstention added to the difficulties of the Crown, for the calmer and more judicial temperaments shrank from office and resigned. Henri de Mesme tells how Catherine visited his house by night closely veiled, and dragged him back to public life. "It was time," she said, "to aid his country. It sat not well on a good citizen to be seated at his ease, shut up in his garden and his study during the hurricane of a nation's storm."

The Crown had little more control over its executive. A few soldiers and statesmen, such as Vielleville and Castelnau, were ready to carry out their orders. Even bigots like Montluc and Tavannes hung disturbers of the peace from either side, but when fighting once began, they were not proof against religious party feeling. Everything depended upon the individual character of governors and lieutenant governors, and minor officials; there was no common custom of obedience. Thus it was that after St. Bartholomew the orders of the Crown, whether for extermination or for pacification, received a different measure of obedience in every province and in every town. Throughout the wars the King was well served by some of the more professional soldiers, but their livelihood depended upon the continuance of the struggle, they could not be sufficiently disinterested to help the nation to peace.

The judicial attitude was thus probably impracticable. Catherine, in marrying her son to the daughter of the emperor Maximilian, may well have hoped to introduce into France the judicial and mediatory policy which the emperor long maintained, and which he earnestly pressed upon Henry III. upon his accession to the throne. Maximilian, however, had the most powerful prince in Germany, the Elector of Saxony, to support him, whereas the Queen-mother had but her Chancellor. The outbreak of the second war may have been due to Huguenots or Catholics; the Crown showed a complete consciousness of innocence which all but entailed its capture. After this it deserted professional for personal feelings, and the change is marked by the retirement of L'Hôpital in 1568. His principles were afterwards urged from the philosophical side by Bodin, but the Crown never really again adopted the purely judicial theory. The nearest approach hereafter was the conduct of Henry III. before and after the Peace of Fleix in 1580. He had real volitions towards peace, but peace with him meant leisure for amusement, and the nation by this time was out of hand.

The second alternative is the history of the international politics of these wars. Under Henry II. France had fought a drawn game against the united powers of Spain and England. It was clear that internal division would render her weaker than the national enemies, and it was natural that soldiers of both confessions should wish to heal internal wounds by the outbreak of external war. It was the Catholic Vielleville who said that the only side which had won at the desperate and doubtful combat of St. Denis was the side of the King of Spain. To the Queen-mother is due the credit of initiating this policy of union. After the first war she cemented the peace by leading both Catholics and Huguenots to turn the English out of Havre. This, however, was an act of merely defensive warfare, and could lead to no permanent result. Catherine had no desire for a breach with England, for she had many interests in common with Elizabeth. Chief of these was the dislike of Mary Stuart, grounded in both cases partly on personal jealousy, partly on political dangers. To both it was essential to traverse the negotiations for a marriage between the Queen of Scotland and Don Carlos, heir to the Spanish monarchy. The union of Spain and Scotland must have been infallibly followed, it was thought, by the absorption of England. France would have become a mere *enclave* in Spanish lands and Spanish waters; and, more than this, the Queen-mother would have been, within her own dominions, at the mercy of the House of Guise. Thus a national war against England was suicidal to both parties, and the Treaty of Troyes re-established friendly relations with the English Court.

This peace by no means implied hostility with Spain. The Court had been assisted by Spanish auxiliaries against the Huguenots. The celebrated interview of Bayonne, between Catherine and the King on one side, and her daughter, the Queen of Spain, and the Duke of Alva on the other, seemed likely to lead to a closer intimacy. Catherine's objects in this interview have always been a subject of dispute. She probably wished to propitiate Philip, alienated by the recent peace with the heretics, to obviate any dangerous connection between him and the more extreme French Catholics, and, above all, to further the dynastic interests of her children—to marry her second daughter Margaret to Don Carlos, and her son Henry to Philip's widowed sister, the Queen of Portugal. The direct result, however, of these relations with Spain was a fresh outbreak of civil war, because the Huguenots were convinced that measures had been concerted at Bayonne for their suppression, and indeed such measures had taken a very prominent place in the debates.

It seemed inevitable that harmony in France should vary in inverse proportion to union between France and Spain.

Philip's pressure upon the French court was caused by no mere abstract zeal for Catholicism. He was aware of the discontent, religious and political, that was smouldering in the Netherlands, he feared that any success of the Huguenots would set it ablaze, and he wished to commit the French government once for all to the Catholic cause, for otherwise it could not fail to take advantage of Low-Country disaffection. Even before the revolt, while Alva was urging Catherine at Bayonne to crush the Huguenots, he was complaining of the reception of a Turkish envoy at Marseilles. From the outbreak of the revolt the mission of the Spanish minister at Paris was to unravel the intrigues with the Protestants or the Turk. Schomberg, the great "recruiting sergeant" of the Crown, himself a Protestant, was as often employed in negotiating Protestant alliances as in raising reiters for the Catholic cause. The outbreak occurred in 1566, but so great was the distrust of the Huguenots for the Crown, that not until 1570 could the French seriously realize its importance to themselves. This, however, was the secret of the Peace of St. Germain. The opportunity had come for recovering the losses of Francis I.'s reign, of again making French influence predominant over the whole possessions of the House of Burgundy, of again entering into relations with the lesser Italian powers to combat the supremacy of Spain. French sailors as well as English cast longing glances at the colonial wealth of Spain. The growing French commerce could expand at the expense of the Spaniard, and this, being chiefly in Huguenot hands, it would give them employment, and divert their attention from religious strife. Subjects of dispute, both personal and national, were not lacking. The Spaniards in 1566 had massacred the French settlers in Florida. Philip had perpetually thwarted Catherine in her dynastic schemes; he had refused his sister to Henry, his son to Margaret; he had prevented the latter likewise from marrying the King of Portugal; he had consoled himself for the death of Elizabeth of France by filching from her brother Charles his intended bride, the elder daughter cf the emperor. He was threatening the absorption of Siena in his Italian possessions; he was attempting to detach the Swiss from their traditional alliance with the French crown. Charles IX., jealous of his brother's triumphs in the civil war, had an access of warlike zeal, and was burning to eclipse them on a more creditable field. The main points for consideration were, How far could the French crown openly interfere in the struggle between Philip and his subjects, and how far in so doing would it be committed to the Huguenots in France? What, moreover, would be the attitude of England towards a French invasion of Flanders, and with what amount of favour would the Catholic government of France be regarded by the rebels in the Netherlands?

There could at all events be no doubt as to the welcome accorded by the Prince of Orange to the assistance of the French crown. He had realised from the first that success with a purely religious programme was impossible. The elements of Protestantism were too scattered geographically, and too divided ecclesiastically, to render possible a great Protestant system of alliance. In the Netherlands themselves the revolt comprised the most irreconcileable elements. In Holland was an aristocratic commercial bourgeoisie with Erastian principles, jealous of foreign interference, incapable of combined action, yet acting with self-sacrifice in local self defence. Beneath it were urban populations, sometimes Catholic, sometimes Calvinist. The majority of the country population, probably in Holland, and certainly in the inland northern provinces, was Catholic. In Antwerp, the commercial capital of the Netherlands, Catholics, Lutherans, Calvinists, and Anabaptists were intermingled, the Lutherans tending to unite with the Catholics, and the lower section of the Calvinists with the Anabaptists. In the manufacturing centres of Flanders and Brabant were urban democracies, violent in political and religious proselytism, forming municipal fed-

H

erations, taking the offensive against noble and Catholic elements, pressing at one moment for a centralised unity, at another for a cantonal federation; among them occasional aristocracies, as at Bruges, or at all events an upper bourgeoisie which was often Catholic, as in Holland it was Erastian. In Hainault, Artois, Limburg, and Luxemburg, was a rural population with a Catholic nobility, inclined to monarchy yet resenting its exclusion under the Granvelle Government from monarchical administration. Yet side by side with these nobles were towns with a large Calvinist element, such as Arras, Lille, and Valenciennes, backed by considerable Reformed populations in territories geographically, but not politically, Netherland—Maestricht, Liege, and Cambrai.

The only possible bond of union was resistance to Spanish garrisons, and Spanish maladministration, and the only possible resource a political rival of Spain, and a European war not religious but political.

This was Orange's objection to the English alliance, which his supporters, the Dutch, preferred. There was no political jealousy between England and Spain; it was with difficulty that England broke away from its Spanish relations, to which it was constantly returning. English intervention implied that the more religious section of the government (the Walsingham or Leicester section) had obtained the upper hand, and intervention of a purely religious order he avoided. Hence also he disliked a purely Huguenot connection, apart from the geographical difficulties to its realisation. The Crown of France was the natural rival of Spain, the traditional non-Protestant ally of Protestant peoples; a power which might readily attach the provinces of the South, and not be dangerous to those of the North; which might bring with it support from England of a not exclusively religious colour. If France could be made to break with Spain, the independence of the Netherlands was possible. The whole question turned upon the elimination of the religious factor as far as possible from Netherland politics, and entirely from international politics.

Naturally enough there were early negotiations between the French Court and Orange, and his correspondents are Catherine and the Constable, and not the Huguenots, unless they are in favour at Court.

As early as 1563-4 Orange was corresponding with the Queen. In January 1566 the King declared that he would some day enforce his claims to Flanders. Throughout this year, and the next, Orange was in constant communication with the Queen-mother and the Constable, and D'Andelot acted as agent for the Gueux at Court. The attempt of Genlis on Cambrai was made with the cognisance of the French Crown.

On the outbreak of the war in 1567 Orange refused to join Condé. Forced into France in 1568 by Alva, he was not attacked by the royal troops, who might easily have annihilated him. Catherine's negotiations with him were the subject of constant representations from the Spanish minister Alava. The aggressive Catholic policy of the Crown in 1568-9 forced Orange indeed into alliance with the Huguenots, but he submitted to the stigma of personal cowardice rather than commit himself against the Crown, and he played an important part in the Treaty of St. Germain, though out of favour with the Huguenot party.

From this moment his connection with the royal family never ceased until his death. But it was his more adventurous brother Louis who personally brought matters to a crisis. He had for some time been carrying on depredations upon Spanish commerce, in conjunction with the people of Rochelle. He was now brought by Coligni's son-in-law Teligni to an interview with the King. He unfolded a brilliant prospect before the dazzled eyes of Charles. Flanders and Artois should be once more incorporated with France; the German princes would be tempted by the promise of Brabant and Guelders, Luxemburg and Limburg; England by that of Holland and Zealand.

The attitude of England was uncertain. France could not engage in war with Spain without covering herself by an English alliance, and yet nothing England dreaded more than a French advance on Antwerp. Elizabeth plainly said that she would sooner see the Spaniards there than the French, the possession of Holland and Zealand would hardly have compensated her for the dangers of the French command of Flanders and the great city of the Scheldt. More favourable to England was a proposal for an independent sovereignty of the Netherlands for a French prince who should be wedded to the English queen. Catherine had formerly proposed a marriage between Elizabeth and Charles IX., she now offered the Duke of Anjou, who should be sovereign of the Netherlands, and possibly the future emperor. But the negotiations broke down on the insuperable objections of Anjou. An arrangement was indeed arrived at in the treaty of Blois, but this was of the nature of a merely defensive alliance, and did not prevent the English government from listening to the commercial overtures of Alva.

Meanwhile events moved rapidly. The rebel ships expelled from Dover surprised Brill and Flushing. Louis of Nassau left the Court, and with aid secretly supplied by the French King seized Mons and Valenciennes. Elizabeth, not to be outdone, allowed English volunteers to cross to Flushing. French emissaries were busy in Italy and Germany, and a common scheme of action was arranged with the Porte. The eagerly desired vacancy in Poland occurred at this propitious moment, and Anjou's candidature found favour both in Poland and Germany. France seemed likely to head a combination against the two branches of the house of Hapsburg. The aid given by Charles to Louis of Nassau had been discovered by the Spanish Court, and war was certain. Troops were being openly levied in France and Switzerland, of which Coligni was to take command. The French fleet under Strozzi was preparing to sail for the Channel. The Huguenot nobility had flocked to Paris. Delay was only caused by the marriage of Catherine's daughter, Margaret, to Henry of Navarre, and it was significant that this was solemnized without waiting for the Pope's dispensation. Then, of a moment, the attempt on Coligni and the massacre of St. Bartholomew stopped the pulse of war. The causes of this extraordinary tragedy will be for all time a source of dispute, and here they can be only lightly touched. There were present three distinct factors, the old feud between Guises and Châtillons, accentuated by Coligni's supposed connivance at the murder of Duke Francis, the bloodthirsty hatred of the Catholic populace of Paris for the Huguenot nobility, which merely needed that the government should withdraw its hand, and the personal feelings of the Queen-mother.

How then was Catherine induced to surrender in a moment the fruits of her elaborate diplomacy? She had at once a constitutional liking for diplomatic intrigue, and a nervous horror of war. Consequently more than once she shrank back from the conflict which her aggressive policy had done much to kindle. She had now perhaps rightly estimated the possibilities of failure. La Noue had been driven from Valenciennes; the succour which was forwarded to Louis of Nassau, under Genlis, was cut to pieces in an ambuscade. Letters which compromised the French King came into Alva's hands. The experienced governors of Picardy and Burgundy warned her that they were in no condition to fight Spain. News arrived from Genoa that Spanish troops were being massed in Italy, to be thrown upon the southern provinces of France. Venice sent her most experienced envoy, Michieli, to entreat the French king not to break with Spain, and so baulk continued success against the Turk; and Catherine was peculiarly open to the influence of Italian diplomats. Above all, the action of Elizabeth, on whose co-operation everything depended, was undeniably ambiguous; it was believed that she was preparing to betray Flushing to the Spaniards. But Catherine had more personal motives than these. Her dominant passion was influence, and in war the influence of a woman and a diplomatist was gone. It was in fact gone already; for once her son had broken away from her guidance; Coligni was dragging him into wars in defiance of his mother's counsels. Coligni Catherine disliked above all the party leaders, and she believed that since Condé's death the political existence of the Huguenot party depended on him alone. Were he dead, these wild schemes of war would drop, and the Queen would recover her control.

The question of premeditation is very difficult. There is no doubt that ever since the outbreak of the troubles the possibility of sacrificing the chiefs of the Huguenots was present to Catherine. Alva and the Duke of Montpensier alike had at Bayonne urged upon her the laying low of four or five heads, and there is evidence to prove that these words were ever since ringing in her ears. Yet she had before this missed opportunities, and but for sudden passion the floating idea might never have been executed. Cool and skilful as she was, she lost her head, overmastered by jealousy and fear, the two surest incentives to bloodshed. Had the shot from behind the curtain struck home, the tragedy might have closed with the Admiral's death. But he stooped to adjust his stirrup, and received a wound not likely to be fatal. The outspoken threats of the Huguenots, the indignation of the King, his apparent determination to track out the murderers, and the fear of immediate discovery, converted the Queen's previous fears into panic terror, and hence the resolve to drown her guilt in the blood of the whole party.

The personal hatred of the Guises, and the rabid Catholic zeal of the Parisians, were instruments which Catherine, or any other, could have employed at any moment. Her one difficulty was to stifle the honour, and stimulate the fear, of the unfortunate young King.

Such seems the most probable explanation of one of

history's most pitiful tragedies. Yet the Huguenots have always believed that St. Bartholomew was the fruit that had been ripening since Bayonne, and throughout Europe, from the moment of the advent of the Huguenots to Paris, there was presentiment of some great horror. Of the two Venetian envoys, the more experienced believed in premeditation, the other thought that the execution was so imperfect, so ill-timed, so bungling, that it was the work of momentary passion. It is certain that the Court had never decided upon its future course, and within a few days three contradictory statements were put forth. The world was told that an *émeute* had occurred between the Guises and the Châtillons which the government had suppressed. Then secret orders were sent to the provinces that the King was resolved to exterminate the Huguenots. Finally it was published that the Crown had been forced to forestall a political plot against itself, and that no change would be made in its relations to the Admiral's peaceful co-religionists. The effect upon foreign politics was immediate. The Pope and the King of Spain naturally believed that France was now pledged to Catholicism. Elizabeth rejected Catherine's advances and turned towards Spain. The Emperor converted his genuine horror to diplomatic uses, emphasizing to Poles and Germans the part played in the tragedy by Henry of Anjou. Yet Catherine was not discouraged; she had never intended a total change of policy either within France or without. She had recovered the reins. She intended the direction to be the same, but the pace not so break-neck. Without France she succeeded. In a few months Henry was elected to the throne of Poland; was received with honour, and escorted on his road by the most uncompromising of German Calvinists. A Roman envoy had in vain dangled his heels at Paris, and been finally dismissed with marked discourtesy. Philip was again threatened by a combination between France, England, and his revolted subjects. Elizabeth had, after three months, consented to act as godmother to Charles' daughter, and was listening favourably to Alençon's proposals. Within a week Orange had renewed his negotiations with the French Crown, and was receiving subsidies from the hand which he had declared could never be cleansed from the blood of St. Bartholomew. Yet the crime had brought its punishment, for this success abroad was rendered futile by the loss of unity at home. France could be no longer an object of hope and fear, when the Crown was breaking its strength against the walls of Rochelle and Sancerre; when great part of the southern provinces, Catholic as well as Protestant, were preparing to withdraw from practical allegiance.

The death of Charles and the return of Henry from Poland further complicated the foreign policy of the Crown. Catherine, though she still wielded enormous influence, was no longer absolute, for the King took other counsellors than his mother. Moreover, between Henry and his brother Alençon-Anjou there existed a jealousy amounting to hatred. The younger brother had no deep religious convictions, but he turned towards the Huguenots as being the more stirring military party, their aid could give him an independent power within the state, and a self-sufficing sovereignty abroad. Affecting to despise the luxury and effeminacy of the Court, he posed as the military leader of the nation, and gladly surrounded himself with its professional captains, independent of creed. Jealousy, natural predilection, and self interest all pointed to the frontiers. At once headstrong, impatient, and irresolute, he would adopt any scheme that appeared adventurous, and on the first check exchange it for another. The Queen-mother was ambitious to win a crown for her younger son. She saw with anguish that the two brothers could not live at peace, and that every quarrel might cause a fresh breach between the two religious parties. Thus she too pushed her son towards the Netherlands, while shrinking from open conflict with the Spaniard. The King perpetually wavered; now jealous of his brother's success, now craving to be rid of him, unable altogether to let slip the opportunities which rebellion against Spain offered to the French monarchy, yet revolting against a combination with Calvinist rebels against a friendly Catholic power. Thus in the ten years between 1574–1584, it is difficult at any moment to estimate the exact responsibility of the Crown in the intrigues with the Netherlands. Alençon at all events becomes the centre of interest rather than the King. Religiously colourless, he was characteristically French; his very failings and inconsequences endeared him to diplomatic agents, he was the golden calf set up for the golden age of diplomacy to worship. To Orange, Alençon was indispensable. He hoped that circumstances would force the French prince into the policy of toleration, which he himself adopted from conviction, for his importance in France rested solely on his command of a combined Politique-Huguenot party. It was such a party that Orange wished to create in the Netherlands. He had in fact no alternative. The French would not have suffered English presence in West Flanders and Artois, the Walloon nobles would not have submitted to his own supremacy. The Catholic majority in the southern provinces would not have obeyed any but a Catholic chief. The influence of Orange was always in inverse proportion to that of the religious factor. This is true of his position within the Netherlands and without, and it is this which indissolubly connects his fortunes with those of Alençon. The connection between events in France and in the Netherlands was closest when religious considerations and revolutionary principles were least prominent.

St. Bartholomew had caused only a momentary breach in the relations of Orange with the French Crown. The terms arranged at the Fair of Frankfort, by which the southern provinces of the Netherlands were abandoned to French conquest, marks the beginning of the second stage of negotiations. The marriage of Orange with the Huguenot ex-abbess of Jouarre, Charlotte of Montpensier, is often regarded as the sign of *rapprochement* towards the Huguenots. Yet it was negotiated by the Queen-mother, who made herself responsible for the dowry, and engaged to reconcile the bride's father. The more nearly France was inclined to Spain, as in 1572 and 1576, the more ready was Orange to negotiate, and the higher were his bids. English jealousy was still the difficulty. Notwithstanding her negotiations for marriage with Alençon, Elizabeth on the whole leant towards Spain from St. Bartholomew until the end of 1576, or even 1578, especially during the milder administration of Requesens. She believed that the massacre would be followed by a Catholic movement from France in favour of Mary Stuart, and indeed Henry III. returned from Poland with the avowed intention of restoring her. Thus the English queen constantly intrigued not only with Spain, but with the extreme Huguenots, and with the adventurous son of the Elector Palatine, John Casimir, who wished to assume the lead of an aggressive European Calvinist combination. Her desire was to mediate in the Netherlands, to reinstate a tolerant but weak administration under the mere suzerainty of Spain, such as would not interfere with the development of her own carrying trade, which she was consciously striving to convert into a monopoly. But the intrigues of Don John of Austria, the new governor of the Netherlands, with Mary Stuart, and of Alençon with Philip II., alarmed Elizabeth, and in 1578 the negotiations began which ended in her betrothal with the French prince.

If fear of England had checked a French advance upon the Netherlands, the fear of Spain was also a deterrent. Alençon thought that he might gain the sovereignty under Spanish suzerainty by means of a Spanish marriage. This probably accounted for his momentary outburst of Catholic zeal at the Estates of Blois in 1576-7. He could only execute his designs by a Spanish marriage, and with the help of the zealous Catholics, or by sharing the spoil with Elizabeth.

Till the day of his death he wavered between these alternatives. Twice did Alençon appear upon the Netherland stage. The farce preceded the tragedy. In 1578 he entered the country at the request of the Catholic nobility of Hainault disgusted with the religious and political proselytism of the Flemish sectaries, but disinclined as yet to revert to Spain. Orange and the States-General stood aloof, for he brought no guarantee of royal aid. Elizabeth in alarm subsidised John Casimir to act as a check upon the French. Thus there were three forces all opposed to Spain, yet all secretly hostile to each other. It was not known how far the French Crown was involved, it was long doubted whether Alençon would not combine with Don John against the Estates. Don John's death relieved the pressure. Hostilities broke out between Walloons and Flemings, and Alençon threatened to head the former, and create an independent Walloon principality. But his forces disbanded themselves, his Calvinist mercenaries slipping over the lines to join Casimir, and his French Catholics deserting to the Catholic malcontents. In 1579 Alençon and John Casimir both disappeared. The line of division again became religious, it had proved impossible to adopt at once a Catholic and an anti-Spanish programme. The more Protestant provinces consolidated themselves in the union of Utrecht, while Artois and Hainault coalesced in the union of Arras, and renewed their allegiance to Spain.

More serious was the invasion of 1581. Parma's successes, and the union of Arras, had forced Orange again to revert to France. By the Treaty of Plessis the sovereignty of the Netherlands had been accorded to Alençon and his heirs, subject to guarantees against their incorporation with France by his succession to the throne, or with Spain by a Spanish marriage. But Alençon must be no private adventurer; he must bring with him a definite pledge of support and recognition from the Crown, and this was given.

Henry recognised his brother's sovereignty, and secretly

engaged to furnish troops. As compensation the province of Artois was promised to the Crown. France seemed definitely to have started on the career of conquest. Elizabeth's opposition was, it was hoped, disarmed; the negotiations for her betrothal with Alençon were pushed to a conclusion. The European Catholic system was to be shattered by the alliance of the Protestant and the Politique powers, by the creation of an independent Franco-English principality in the Netherlands. With the view of a fresh invasion Cambrai had been occupied, and the Peace of Fleix concluded. A French fleet sailed to create a diversion against Spain, on the side of Portugal, giving support to the shadowy Pretender, Antonio, Prior of Crato.

Yet from the first Alençon tried to get from Philip recognition of his title as Duke of Brabant. His attempt to raise Huguenot levies failed; the Estates of Holland and Zealand never gave real recognition to a Catholic and a Frenchman. The sectaries, after their first enthusiastic welcome, intensified his Catholicism and that of his troops by their fanatical insolence. He had lost his Catholic adherents in Hainault and Artois, who now concurred in the recall of Spanish troops. He was constantly baulked by English jealousy; hence his design to fortify his position by violence, and his treacherous attempt upon Antwerp and other towns. Of this, if not the King, Catherine at least was cognisant, and pushed forward large reinforcements. It was an attempt at the conquest of the southern provinces, which would have forced Spain to effect a compromise.

Alençon's ignominious failure at Antwerp was the climax of the endeavours to turn French arms abroad. Negotiations indeed did not cease, and it was after the death both of Orange and of Alençon that the sovereignty of the Netherlands was offered to the French Crown itself. But Henry could not accept this proposal, because the religious factor was again becoming all important. The diversion towards the Netherlands had indeed thrice stopped the course of war against the Huguenots; to it had been due the Peace of Monsieur, that of Bergerac, and that of Fleix. But the storm had gathered in another quarter, and this tampering with the Protestant rebels of a Catholic king was a main cause of the outburst of the League.

The French royal family had failed in its timid and tentative adoption of the second alternative—the lead of the nation against the foreigner. The treacherous French aid had apparently riveted the Spanish chains upon the Netherlands. Even had Orange lived he could not have saved the southern provinces. Yet his failure was not so complete as that of his ally. He had committed the French Crown to hostility with Spain. Philip's manipulation of the League was the revenge for the aid given to his rebels. The French Court dreaded a more direct attack. It was paralysed with fear as it watched the Armada off its coasts. It was very generally believed that it was intended, with the aid of the League, to occupy French ports. Great was the rejoicing of the royalists at the ruin of the Spanish fleet. Even the very Catholic Parisians could not forbear to jeer. Notices were placarded in the street—"Lost, somewhere off the English coast, the magnificent Armada. Anyone bringing information of its whereabouts to the Spanish Embassy shall receive five crowns reward."

"God has deferred our ruin," wrote the Tuscan agent Cavriana, "contenting Himself with our torments of civil war, and suffering Philip's design to be frustrated, for his Armada, cast upon the Orkneys, tattered and torn, has returned to Spain without harming any one in the world except itself."

But the danger to the Crown was not over, although he who wielded the sceptre was a king of different calibre. Parma's two invasions of France were in reality the counterblows for the invasions of Alençon. And it was these invasions that saved the northern provinces of the Netherlands, by diverting the Spanish troops when there were no means of substantial resistance left. They saved, moreover, the cause of Henry of Navarre, and the existence of Reform in France, for the bulk of the nation was at length brought to realize that it was engaged in a foreign war, and that religious antipathy must for the time give place to national sympathies. Before long the French Crown would be again able to reassume the offensive. The political system of Henry IV. was no new departure, but the natural and necessary outcome of thirty years of French diplomacy, postponed only by furious outbreaks of civil war. Henry differed from Alençon and Catherine not so much in his aims as in his competency. It is due to the despised Italian to remember that her ships were destroyed off the Azores in the only attempt made to save Portugal from Spain, and that, nervous, half-hearted, and treacherous as she was, to her repeated efforts the humiliation of Spain in the Netherlands was in some measure due.

It was not unnatural that the Crown should place itself at the head of one or other of the religious parties. Kings and queens have after all their personal religious feelings, and are liable with their subjects to epidemics of intolerance. The personal religion of Charles V., of Mary of England, even of Elizabeth, had no inconsiderable bearing upon the fortunes of the Reformation. Yet in France the opinions of the Crown had little effect upon the progress of events. It may be said that the Crown never voluntarily placed itself at the head of either religious party. Before the wars began, indeed, it seemed as though Catherine would balance the power of the Guises by assuming the lead of the new movement. Calvinist hymns and doctrines became the fashion at the Court. The sermons of the Court preacher Montluc were so unorthodox that they are said to have driven the Constable over to the Guises. The Queen herself advised the Pope to make concessions, to order the removal of images from the altars, to modify baptismal rites, to grant communion in two kinds, to abolish private masses, to chant the Psalms in French, to suppress the *fête* of the Sacrament. It seems indubitable that she gave encouragement to the Huguenots in their first rising, and it was with the greatest reluctance that she and the young King were dragged into the Catholic camp. The murder of Duke of Guise delighted no one more than Catherine, for it freed the Crown from the shackles of a religious party. She stubbornly resisted Alva's pressure to place the Crown at the head of the Catholics. Bitterly offended by the attempt of the Huguenots to secure their persons in the second war, Catherine and her son for a moment adopted a Catholic attitude in the third war; yet the Queen was soon willing to grant the Huguenots better terms than they cared to accept, that she might escape from her position. Apart from personal motives, it was the fear that the Crown was associating itself too closely with the Reformed party that drove Catherine to St. Bartholomew. Yet she never admitted that this committed her to the Catholic party, though she could for the moment utilise it with the more safety because all the great Catholic leaders had disappeared. She took the earliest opportunity of dissociating the Crown from pure party leadership. The Huguenots naturally disbelieved her, yet she was really anxious again to assume a middle because an independent position.

Henry III. might more naturally have taken up the *rôle* of party leader. He was a zealous, at times a fanatic, Catholic. He had as Duke of Anjou won great successes as a party chief, had been under the guidance of one of the great party men, Tavannes. He might naturally hope to be the first man among the Catholics, especially as the Cardinal of Lorraine died almost immediately after his accession. It was suspected, indeed, that Catherine intended to control both parties by putting one brother at the head of each. But just at this moment party feeling seemed almost worn out; the party of compromise was to all appearance the strongest at Court, and it may be said that the Peace of Monsieur forced Henry out of the position of a party chief. Then came the awakening of the Catholic masses which culminated in the League. Henry must either head and direct the League himself, or must show himself so zealous a Catholic that there is no reason for a League, he must outbid the League. This he attempted to do at the Estates of Blois. He wished the Estates to give a formal sanction to his position as head of the Catholics for the express purpose of crushing the Huguenots. He succeeded in so far that he prevented the League from completely controlling the Estates, as it had expected. But he failed, because while the Catholics could find money for the war, the State could find none, and because while Henry had lost all credit with the zealots, the Duke of Guise was captivating the Catholic masses. Hence Henry was forced to join the League in the vain hope of leading it. He did indeed see the other alternative, that of leaving the platform of party leader, and of adopting the middle position, and towards this he made some effort, which is marked by the Peace of Fleix. When, however, this course necessitated the recognition of Navarre as heir, he felt that it would cost him the crown. The day of the Barricades compelled him to throw in his lot with the League; but this implied the abeyance of the Crown, it was no longer a free agent. From this thraldom Henry hoped to escape by the murder of the Duke of Guise and his brother. The assassination drove him into his professional position, and it is characteristic that the most Catholic of French kings was murdered while leading a combined host of Catholics and Huguenots in the cause of toleration and legitimate succession.

The creation of a third or Royalist party to balance those of the Bourbons and the Guises, was a natural resource of the afflicted Monarchy. It had been urged upon Catherine from the first by Marshal Tavannes. It had been the policy, in similar emergencies, of Charles V., of Charles VII., and of Louis XI. It was the key to the policy of Henry III., being partly the cause and partly the effect of his favouritism. The old marshal, however, had believed that the Monarchy might find support in nobility just under the first rank, possessing great provincial influence, as yet uncorrupted by Court life, still able to produce the first soldiers and statesmen of France. Henry's favourites were, on the other hand, recommended purely by their personal beauty, their taste in dress, or at most by their skill in duelling, which became the mania of the Court. They brought to the King no talent, no provincial support. Moreover this third party rested on a false principle; it was based upon attachment to the king as a man, rather than on loyalty to the King as a ruler. The favourites stood in an entirely different relation to Henry to that held by the few professional generals and statesmen who adhered to him.

The King instead of gathering fresh force into his own hands was giving what was left to him away. Most of the favourites were unimportant from a political point of view, except as bringing to a blaze all the smouldering odium against the Coürt. But the powers conferred on La Valette, Duke of Epernon, and Arques, Duke of Joyeuse, formed a deliberate attempt to create fresh magnates, whose power might exceed that of the leaders of the Catholic and Huguenot parties.

No mere subject had ever possessed the powers which Epernon amassed after the death of his rival Joyeuse at Coutras. Duke of Epernon and Peer of France, Admiral and Colonel-General of Infantry, he controlled the governments of Normandy, Provence, Angoulême, Saintonge, Boulogne, and Metz, holding, it was observed, the keys of France, for the King held him to be their safest keeper. Sole gentleman of the Chamber, sole governor of his master's opinions and caprices, he was as absolute at Court as in his provinces—every ambassador must interview Epernon before he was granted audience.

It is clear that even if Henry III. could depend on the personal attachment of these favourites, and the result proved that this was not certain, they would necessarily be as dangerous to his successors as were the older magnates to himself. It was the last resource of a disintegrating monarchy. Moreover the favourites, selected on personal rather than on professional grounds were themselves apt to be engulfed by the religious or political parties. Thus Joyeuse drifted from the King's side toward the League, of which his family became among the most extreme supporters. Epernon, on the other hand, was rightly suspected of intimate relations with the Huguenots and Politiques of the South, especially with Damville. That the relationship was purely personal, and not professional, is proved by the fact that in the royal family itself there were several groups of such favourites. The Queen-mother had her separate party, whilst Alençon lived within his vast appanage in more than royal state, surrounded by favourites nearly as objectionable as were the King's. Each group moreover had frequent dissensions within itself. In this "Court of silk and blood" duelling was draining the hot blood of France. It was costing more lives, writes Tavannes, than many a pitched battle. One of the dangers of the system was its apparent resemblance to the formation of a royal party properly so called. Yet the difference was clearly recognised. A union between Catholics and Huguenots to crush the Politiques was inconceivable, but La Noue did recommend a combination of the two religions to crush the favourites, and Henry of Guise made a similar proposal to the Huguenots. Even in Paris a distinction was preserved. When the Revolution broke out the Politiques were watched, but the King's friends were imprisoned. From Provincial Estates and Estates General alike came the cry for the humiliation of the favourites. Even Damville's enemies would have regarded his governorship of Languedoc as resting on a different basis to Epernon's rule in Normandy and Provence. Finally the death of Henry III. made the position of the favourites yet more obvious, for not a few, and among them

Epernon, deserted the Crown and joined their religious party. This for a Politique would have been impossible. Yet it is not always easy in individual cases to draw a line between the Politique and the member of the Court party. "By their fruits ye shall know them." After Henry of Navarre's accession the Politique was his surest adherent, the member of the Court party his most troublesome opponent. The crime and error of Henry III. had been not to extend a welcome to the moderate Catholics, who already in the South formed an organised party. This was the natural Royalist party which was forced by the action of the Crown into opposition. So also the floating mass of Royalist opinion in Northern and Central France found no solid ground to which to adhere, until it was gradually concentrated by the outburst of the Revolution. Thus when the crisis came the Monarchy was desolate, it could help neither itself nor others. "All the kingdom is in arms," wrote the Tuscan Cavriana in June, 1588, "the peasants are desperate, close their villages, fortify themselves against the troops of both parties, and die of famine; they will pay no taxes direct or indirect. The cities form themselves into republics, and gather round the Guises. The nobility is divided, and passes now to this faction, now to that. Justice is completely dead. France is parted into two—the Leaguers, and the adherents of the House of Bourbon. The former have complete command of this side of the Loire, the latter of the other. The King is naked and alone, and can give us no redress."*

With the death of Henry III. the shilly-shally of the Crown was at an end. Whatever might be the case with the nation the legitimate monarch was at all events at open war with the foreigner, though it was not technically declared until 1595. The patriots must with time inevitably gather round the King. It was equally clear that Navarre was no mere leader of a religious party; his forces consisted as much of

* DESJARDINS, IV. 744.

Catholics as Huguenots. He was believed to be indifferent as to doctrine. Keen observers had long foreseen that his abjuration of heresy was merely a matter of opportunity. Coming though he did from the Huguenot ranks, Henry was the Politique *par excellence*, the natural leader of all who " preferred the safety of their country to the salvation of their soul."

Mr. Besant has said that the Reformation failed because it was deserted by the Renaissance, by the philosophers, the scholars, the divines, the men of broad modern views. In Henry of Navarre they could once more find a rallying point. The more serious could have had no sympathy with the loathsome morals, the aimless bloodshed, the senseless frivolity of the Valois Court; while the more intellectual were disgusted by the fits of repentant bigotry of the King, and yet more by the uneducated fanaticism of the League. But Navarre's formal orthodoxy covered a tolerance as wide as their own. He was no scholar, but he could talk and write as well as he fought. He combined the dignity of the Bourbon with the witty banter of the Gascon. His despatches, his manifestos, his letters, were so many victories. His impudent reply to his excommunication had won the sympathies of Sixtus V. himself. Long before his entry into Paris his witticisms at the expense of the League were the delight of the street corner. Satire was a real power, and satire, which had turned against royalty, against Catherine and Henry III., had no hold upon a King who could give more than he received. Satire turned against the League. The moment had perhaps come at last when opinion was outweighing the sword. Yet the sword had necessarily been Navarre's chief instrument. He was incomparably the best French general in the field, and his lieutenants, Biron and Lesdiguières, probably stood next. The Duke of Parma had proved himself tactically Henry's superior, but not strategically. He had driven Henry from both Paris and Rouen, yet Henry closed upon them again as soon as he had turned his back.

His iron grasp upon Paris with but scanty forces did as much credit to his tactics as discredit to the passive cowardice of the citizens. Henry had an instinct for the vital points, the seizure of which was all important; and hence on many an occasion his apparent and much-criticised audacity. He must secure the gastronomic keys to Paris,* Chartres, Rouen, and the Marne; and its military keys, Orleans and the Loire, Amiens and the Somme. Nor was the credit all his own. The old French troops were by this time excellent, and these, whether Huguenot, United Catholic, or professional, were mostly upon Henry's side. The bourgeois militia of the League made a poor show, except when behind walls. On the last German invasion the march and escape of the Huguenot horse was regarded as a model of military pluck and skill. While the Germans were cut to pieces, the Huguenots made a circuit of the whole of France, and got through unhurt. Paris, with 60,000 fighting men, preferred to be starved, to marching out against Henry's 15,000, bivouacked in detachments in the environs.

Henry, if he could wield the sword, the pen, and the tongue showed full appreciation of the purse. He was not scrupulous as to means; while strangling with one hand he would bribe with the other. He bought his enemies in detail. He would not treat with any official representative of the League, for it would have left him face to face with a power equal to himself. His system was longer, but it was more effectual. He bought his political opponents at the expense of the treasury or the State, by governorships or assignations on the taxes. "Render unto Cæsar the things that are Caesar's" was the cynical remark of the Leaguer governor of Paris, as the Leaguer Prevôt des Marchands brought the keys to Henry. "Render, but not sell," was the more zealous Catholic's reply. Religious opponents Henry bought at the expense of the Huguenots by

---

* Thus after Ivry, L'Estoile writes of the capture of Melun, Corbeil, Montereau, and Lagni, "les clefs des vivres de Paris."

religious concessions, excluding Huguenot worship from the district. He would promise everything to the Frenchman, but nothing to the foreigner; he would give nothing that he believed to be the nation's, but everything that he considered to be his own, down to his own conscience. The better men of the Catholic party blamed him but were grateful.

The acceptance of the mass gave Henry Paris, and Paris gave him France. Yet what a France it was to rule! Mayenne with Spanish troops occupied Burgundy and many of the eastern fortresses. Champagne was held by Guise, and coveted by Lorraine, who already was in possession of the Three Bishoprics, the conquest of Henry II. The Duke of Savoy was threatening Dauphiné, and was accepted by part of Provence. Marseilles was an independent republic coquetting with Spain, Lyons an independent principality under the Savoyard Duke of Nemours. The Duke of Tuscany held in mortgage the islands off Provence, and was threatening to extend his security to the mainland. The Pope was advised that Provence would be a useful appendage to Avignon. Joyeuse exercised independent sway in Catholic Languedoc, Villars in Guyenne. Mercœur, resting on Spanish aid, was establishing an independent Duchy of Brittany. The Spaniards surprised Amiens and Calais, the landward and seaward gates of northern France. It cost four years to evict the foreigner, and to receive the submission of the grandees; and the latter too often meant that *de facto* was exchanged for *de jure* independence; the Leaguer Joyeuse for instance was left as governor in Languedoc, side by side with the staunch royalist Damville. The reconciliation of enemies implied the estrangement of allies; Epernon was driven into revolt by the grant of Provence to Guise. The towns, writes Tavannes, were aiming at republican separatism, the nobles at independent tetrarchies. The ambition of the grandees was proved by the proposal of one of the faithful, when French resources were strained to the uttermost by the Spanish capture of

Calais; the governments held under commission should be converted into hereditary properties, the Crown reserving only *homage lige*, and abandoning the national for the feudal military system. The Huguenots formed a republic within a monarchy, half hostile to it, and wholly hostile to its supporters. The recognition of Henry by the Leaguers took the form of a bundle of treaties between the King and individual nobles and individual towns. The monarchy was compared to a ripe pomegranate of which one could see all the grains. And worse than all the State was bankrupt, the revenue wholly inadequate to the expenditure, while an enormous debt had been piled up by the Valois, and increased by subsidies to English, Dutch, Swiss, and Germans, and by the sums for which Leaguer towns and nobles had been bought.

Nevertheless the hour had come for the revival of the French Monarchy, and the hour had brought the man. It was of especial importance that the new King came of a fresh stock, that he had not the heritage of hate and contempt incurred by the extravagance and incapacity of the later Valois. Royalism became the fashion. The anti-monarchical theory had been discredited, abandoned by the Huguenots. stamped out with the League. The Monarchy had fought its last great round with reaction, and tried its first fall with revolution. In both conflicts it had been triumphant. Vanity and fear both bound the nobility to the Crown. They were conscious that to them were mainly due the restoration of the Monarchy and the expulsion of the foreigner; they were enthusiastically royalist and patriotic. Imminent pauperism had mainly driven the gentry to revolt. Secularisation and brigandage had brought more blows than profit. The cry for the revival of worn-out privilege was answered by menaces of extinction. They were lured back to loyalty by the patronage of the Crown, they were frightened to its shelter by the realities of urban democracy and the spectre of agrarian revolt.

The two great rival constitutional institutions of France—the Estates General and the Parliaments—were now silenced before the Crown. The representative system had lost its magic. It was noticed that never had the Estates been so frequently held as during the troubles, and yet the result was nought. "It is a foolish old idea," wrote Pasquier, "that is current among the wisest Frenchmen, that there is nothing which has such power to relieve the people as these assemblies; on the contrary, there is nothing that does them greater mischief, and that for an infinity of reasons." Pasquier indeed was a professional opponent of the Estates; but their champion and apologist, Tavannes, confesses that if a change ever took place in France, it would be effected, not by representative government, but by revolution. Henry, when urged to summon the Estates to meet his financial difficulties, preferred an assembly of notables, which had no constitutional position.

The Judicature indeed proved more long-lived than its rival, yet its strength was sorely shaken. Pasquier noticed that on the same day the King closed the Estates at Blois, and the Revolution closed the State, for such he conceived the Parliament to be, at Paris. The great central Court had suffered terrible indignity; it had been opened and closed at the will of an unauthorised authority; it had been twice purged by the agency of a handful of subordinate officials. One first president had been imprisoned, another hung, and, what was yet more humiliating, the latter had held office while he had protested in secret before two notaries that he regarded his actions as invalid. Repeatedly Parliament had been forced by the Revolution to register edicts against which its conscience and its interest revolted. Its fits of undeniable heroism had availed it as little as its accesses of undoubted cowardice. Its very unity had been broken. As in the days of the English occupation, France saw the royal, judicial, and financial courts in opposite camps, at Paris and at Tours.

The Provincial Parliaments had no less suffered. At Dijon, on the news of Guise's murder, the royalist members had been imprisoned as at Paris. In Normandy and Brittany there were rival courts, each claiming exclusive powers. The Parliament of Toulouse had shamefully surrendered to the mob, had seen the royal arms struck down, had suffered its first president and Advocate-General to be murdered, had been split, not into two, but into three independent courts,* had undergone the stigma of being incapable to preserve a judicial attitude. Henry indeed ultimately owed much to the judicial classes; but the debt was due as much to their fears as to their love. From Huguenots and Catholics alike no cry had been louder than the clamour against the lawyers and their gains. Very apt was the new King's bantering *bon mot*, that his ancestors had feared the Parliaments but did not love them, while he loved them well but did not fear them. This principle was translated into practice, for the Parliaments were forced against their will to register the Edict of Nantes, and the edict establishing the tax upon their incomes did not pass through Parliament at all, but through the Chancery.†

A source of daily annoyance to more loyal and more professional members must have been the daily association with the political upstarts now holding high office under royal commission, as the price of their betrayal of the Revolution.

The Gallican Church at least might seem to have gained by the result of the religious conflict. It had beaten both Huguenot and Pope. It had insisted on a Catholic king, and

---

* At one moment the Royalist section was sitting at Beziers, the Moderate Leaguer at Castel Sarasin, and the Extreme Leaguer at Toulouse. In addition to these was the Mi-partie Chamber, with its complement of Huguenots.

* The establishment of the Paulette, or annual tax, on official incomes, in consideration of which the Crown surrendered the right of sale and the holders acquired an hereditary estate in their offices, is the most curious satire on the grievance which had contributed in no slight degree to bring about the recent troubles.

it had forced Henry to abjuration. On the other hand the French Episcopate, the Catholic Parliaments, even the ultra-Catholic Sorbonne, had all acted in express disobedience to the Pope. Henry reigned by virtue of a title directly opposed to the Papal theory of sovereignty. The dream of an independent Gallican Church was almost realised. There was talk of a French Patriarchate, of the revival of the Pragmatic Sanction. A royal commission made ecclesiastical appointments, and regulated ecclesiastical finance. It was even hoped that a National Council might devise a scheme of doctrine and discipline to reconcile the two religions. But in France Gallicanism was bound up with Constitutionalism. The Pragmatic Sanction tied the hands of the King as fast as it did those of the Pope.

Gallicanism implied the predominance of the Estates, or at least of the ecclesiastical and secular nobility. Moreover hostility to the Pope gave the irreconcileable Leaguers an excuse for fighting with the Spanish armies, a respectable cover for political disloyalty. Thus Henry, as Napoleon, found his interest, not in antagonism to the Papacy, but in a Concordat. But Henry still felt constrained in the presence of the Gallican Church, as he did in that of the Huguenot party. To both he applied the same principle. As he sought to detach a royal party from the more uncompromising Huguenots, and as he hoped to control their ministers by his scheme of concurrent endowment, so he would attach to the Constitutional and National Church an element depending upon royal favour. He recalled the Jesuits, who had been expelled after his attempted assassination by Chastel. Their position in France depended upon royal grace; they had no national support. Parliament, the Sorbonne, the Episcopacy, were all against them. They were to be the religious police of the Bourbon monarchy. To this they were no longer dangerous. Their expulsion had been due to their Spanish sympathies; now they were out of favour with Spain, even threatened with the

Inquisition by their Dominican rivals. Their theocratic-democratic theories were harmless against a King who reigned by Papal and by popular consent, and in their extremest form they had been discouraged.

Thus if Henry IV. was the most national of kings it was not on the religious side. As in politics he played the national factor against the Catholic, so in religion he protected himself against the National Church by the aid of the Castor and Pollux of universal Catholicism—the Pope and the Society of Jesus.

The ground then was levelled for personal monarchy. Parties could be disregarded as well as principles. The grandees, even the Bourbons, were to become an ornament to the Court, not a factor in the Government. Henry's counseller Villeroy said that when there were two parties in a land the King must attach himself to the stronger. Henry replied, No, that he must rule them both. The King's ministers were chosen irrespective of party or antecedents, ability and devotion were the sole qualifications. Of the three chief Sulli was Huguenot, Villeroy an old royalist who had turned Leaguer, Jeannin the chief adviser of Mayenne, and they were never changed. Even the last check on monarchy, the Royal Council, can scarcely be said to have survived, for Henry would ask the advice of its ministers separately, and frequently not take it. Personal government was complete at the centre. In the South alone religious independence, fortified by hardy local privilege and obstinate personal ambition, formed a breach in the absolutism of the Crown.

The League and the Huguenots had run the self-same course. In each there had been the same union between aggrieved towns, pauperised nobles, and ambitious princes, the same jealousy between the several orders, the same programme of constitutional reform, the same pretence of upholding the monarchy, the same levying of war against the King. Each party could be traced far back in the history of the faction fights of the Princes of the Lilies, each had its feudal and its democratic aims, each sacrificed France to the interests of its foreign allies. Neither party deserted its religious principles; but both surrendered their political claims, because both ran counter to the current of national life.

The religious struggle had after all not changed the forces of the constitution, it had but given additional momentum to pre-existing tendencies. The apparent weakness of the monarchy, and the apparent strength of other classes and other institutions, were equally fallacious. How strong the Crown was is proved by the fact that the hated Catherine kept her three despicable sons upon the throne, and that the death of the fourth was regarded as a public calamity that justified revolution. The first of the Bourbons reigned by a title which each party in turn rejected. The new armed prophet of absolutism was one whom the vast majority of France had bound itself by individual oaths never to accept.

Men were not indeed content, but they were weary; they turned languidly to the oldest of all political theories—that the end of government is peace. The sense of all France was expressed in the phrase of the disillusioned Leaguer and Constitutionalist Tavannes, "C'est heur de vivre sous un grand roy, non tyran."

INDEX

Admiral, The. See Châtillon, Coligni.
Aix, Bishop of, 14.
Alava, 99.
Alençon, Duke of, afterwards Anjou, 38–40, 104–110, 114.
Alva, Duke of, 88, 95, 96, 99–102, 111.
Amboise, Peace of, 92.
Amboise, Tumult of, 8, 9, 48.
Amiens, 43, 77, 117, 118.
Angers, 59.
Angoulême, 26, 113.
Anjou, 22.
Anjou, Duke of. See Henry III. and Alençon.
Anne of Beaujeu, 84.
Antonio of Portugal, Prior of Crato, 58, 108.
Antony, King of Navarre, 7, 9, 13, 17, 48, 49.
Antwerp, 3, 97, 100, 108.
Armada, The, 109.
Arras, 3, 98.
Arras, Union of, 107.
Artois, 3, 98, 99, 105, 107, 108.
Aubry, Curé, 66.
Augsburg, Peace of, 2, 43.
Aunis, Estates of, 57.
Auxerre, Bishop of, 66.
Auxerre, Clergy of, 77.
Azores, The, 110.

Badoer, 40.
Balagni, 58.
Barbaro, 32, 88.
Barricades, Day of, 60, 62, 66, 67, 89, 112.
Bastille, The, 67, 69, 76.
Bayonne, 19.
Bayonne, Interview of, 95, 102, 103.
Béarn, 17, 34, 58.
Bergerac, Peace of, 38, 109.
Bèze, Déode de, 4.
Beziers, 22, 121.
Biron, Marshal, 116.
Blois, 63.
Blois, Treaty of, 100.
Bodin, 94.
Bordeaux, 50, 51.
Boucher, Curé, 62, 64, 75.
Bouillon, Duke of, 43, 44.
Boulogne, 113.
Bourbon, Cardinal, "Charles X.," 55, 57, 58, 64, 72, 90.
Bourbon, The Constable, 84.

Bourbon, House of, 7–9, 17, 32, 41, 45, 53, 55, 59, 60, 82, 89, 112, 115, 123, 124.
Bourges, 59.
Brabant, 97, 99.
Bray, Curé of, 4.
Brill, 100.
Brisson, 75.
Brittany, 19, 22, 24, 43, 55, 56, 59, 70, 79, 80, 118, 121.
Bruges, 98.
Burgundy, 22, 24, 53, 56, 59, 76, 96, 101, 118.
Bussi le Clercq, 69, 76.

Caen, 5.
Cahors, 16.
Calais, 27, 46, 85, 118, 119.
Cambrai, 58, 98, 99, 108.
Capuchins, The, 79.
Carcassonne, 16.
Carlos, Don, 55, 95.
Castelnau, 20, 93.
Castel Sarasin, 121.
Castres, 22, 70.
Cateau Cambrésis, Peace of, 5, 7, 28, 46.
Catherine di Medici, 13, 29, 30, 38, 58, 85, 88–90, 92–96, 99–102, 104, 106, 108, 110, 111, 116, 124.
Cavalli, Marino, 49.
Cavriana, 90, 109, 115.
Cevennes, The, 16, 20.
Chalons, 20, 21.
Chambre Ardente, 3, 4.
Chambre des Comptes, 49, 69.
Champagne, 3, 19, 20, 22, 23, 53, 56, 59, 118.
Charles V., Emperor, 10, 110.
Charles V. of France, 112.
Charles VII., 84, 112.
Charles VIII., 5.
Charles IX., 48, 97, 99, 100, 104.
Charles X. See Bourbon, Cardinal.
Chartres, 117.
Chartres, Bishop of, 14.
Chastel, 122.
Châtelet, The, 67.
Châtillon, House of, 7, 13, 18, 59, 101, 103.
Châtillon, Coligni, 7, 8, 16, 18, 26, 30, 33, 48, 62, 85, 86, 92, 99, 100–103.
Châtillon d'Andelot, 7, 8, 99.
Châtillon, Odet, Cardinal, 7, 8, 14.
Clement VII., Pope, 84.
Clément, J., 71, 91.

INDEX.

Cognac, 4.
Comines, Philip de, 10.
Concordat, 10-12, 31, 122.
Condé, Henri, 18, 33, 37-39, 41, 53.
Condé, Louis, 7, 9, 13, 18, 19, 24, 26, 29-31, 48, 58, 86, 99, 102.
Constable, The. See Montmorenci, Anne.
Conti, 41.
Corbeil, 117.
Correr, 11, 19, 28, 87, 88.
Cossé, Marshal, 28.
Cour des Aides, 69.
Courmolet, Curé, 75.
Coutras, Battle of, 59, 113.

Daffis, 70.
D'Aubigné, 43, 62.
Dauphiné, 19-22, 24, 39, 42, 44, 56, 57, 80, 118.
David, 54.
Diana of Poitiers, 7.
Dieppe, 20, 27.
Dijon, 20.
Dominicans, The, 123.
Dreux, Battle of, 18, 23, 49.
Du Plessis Mornay, 35, 43.
Duranti, 70.

Elizabeth of England, 95, 100, 101, 103, 106-108, 110.
Elizabeth of Spain, 95, 96.
Epernon, Duke of, 59, 63, 113-115, 118.
Estates General, 2, 9, 12, 13, 15, 23, 25, 31, 35, 48, 58, 65, 67, 71, 74, 77, 78, 81, 90, 114, 120, 122.
Estates General of Blois, 1576, 52, 54, 106, 112.
Estates General of Blois, 1588, 62, 65, 68, 69, 120.
Estates General of the League, 1593, 76, 80, 82.
Estates General of Orleans, 1561, 16, 30, 73, 76, 85.
Estates of Pontoise, 14, 15, 30, 76.
Etampes, 24.

Flanders, 97, 99, 100, 105.
Fleix, Peace of, 94, 108, 109, 112.
Florida, 96.
Flushing, 100, 101.
Foix, 16.
Fontainebleau, Assembly of, 9.
Forez, The, 22.
Forty, Council General of, 71, 73-75.
Franche-Comté, 47.
Francis I., 26, 29, 45, 46, 77, 79, 96.
Francis II., 8, 13, 26, 29, 45, 48, 55.
Franciscans, The, 4.
Franco-Gallia, The, 35.
Frankfort, Fair of, 105.

Gaetani, Legate, 66, 73.
Gascony, 19.
Gendarmerie, The, 21, 77.
Geneva, 4, 22, 26.
Genlis, 99, 101.
Genoa, 101.

Ghent, 3.
Gondi, The, 47.
Gondi, Archbishop of Paris, 75.
Gonzaga, 47.
Grammont, 19.
Granvelle, 8, 47, 98.
Guelders, 99.
Gueux, The, 28, 99.
Guise, House of, 7, 9, 13, 16, 17, 19, 24, 29, 30, 35, 36, 39-41, 45-48, 52-55, 63, 80, 85, 89, 95, 101-103, 111, 112, 115.
Guise, Duke Claude, 45.
Guise, Duke Francis, 7, 8, 16, 23, 46, 48, 55, 85, 101, 110, 114.
Guise, Duke Henry, 53-62, 67, 69, 72, 80, 86, 89, 90, 112, 121.
Guise, Duke Charles, 79, 118.
Guise, Catherine of. See Montpensier, Duchess of.
Guyenne, 19-21, 24, 26, 34, 42, 56, 118.
Guyenne, Estates of, 52.

Hainault, 3, 98, 107, 108.
Hamilton, Curé, 74.
Hapsburg, House of, 32, 100.
Harlay, President de, 63.
Haton, Claude, 50.
Havre, 27, 85, 94.
Henry II., 3, 6-8, 19, 36, 38, 45, 48, 55, 85, 94, 118.
Henry III., 40, 42, 56, 59, 62, 65, 72, 88, 90, 94-96, 100, 103, 104, 106, 111-116.
Henry IV., 26, 29, 33, 38-46, 57-59, 65, 72, 79, 82, 85, 89, 101, 110, 112, 115, 116, 122, 123.
Holland, 97-100, 108.
Hotman, F., 35.
Hotman, C., 57.

Isle of France, 59.
Ivri, Battle of, 73, 117.

James V. of Scotland, 45, 55.
January, Edict of, 15, 25, 31, 92.
Jarnac, Battle of, 18, 27, 32, 90.
Jeanne d'Albret, Queen of Navarre, 7, 17, 29.
Jeannin, 123.
Jesuits, The, 62, 70, 112, 122, 123.
John, Don of Austria, 106, 107.
John Casimir, Prince Palatine, 38, 39, 106, 107.
Joyeuse, Duke of, 59, 113, 114.
Joyeuse, Henri de, 71, 118.

La Ferté sous Jouarre, Synod of, 35.
Lagni, 117.
La Huguerye, 18, 19.
Languedoc, 19, 22, 24, 34, 37, 42, 59, 71, 114.
Languet, H., 16, 35.
La Noue, 20, 39, 50, 101, 114.
La Rochefoucauld, 19.
La Roue, 75.
La Tremouille, 43.
Leicester, Earl of, 96.
Leo X., Pope, 86.

Le Puy, 20, 67, 71.
Lescar, Bishop of, 14.
Lesdiguières, 116.
L'Estoile, 62, 74, 75, 117.
L'Hôpital, 9, 25, 28, 85, 92, 94.
Liége, 98.
Lille, 3, 98.
Limburg, 98, 99.
Lincestre, Curé, 63.
Lippomano, 86, 87.
Loire, The, 21-24, 43, 44, 59, 115, 117.
Lorraine, Cardinal of, 6, 8, 16, 36, 46, 47, 54, 55, 111, 118.
Lorraine, Duchy of, 7, 45, 47, 85.
Lorraine, Charles, Duke of, 55, 58, 79.
Lorraine, René, Duke of, 45.
Lorraine, House of, 7, 28, 55, 56, 70.
Louis XI., 10, 26, 76, 84, 88, 112.
Louis XII., 10, 45, 55, 77.
Louis XIV., 44, 78, 88.
Louviers, 25.
Louvre, The, 61.
Lovers', The, War, 39.
Luxemberg, 98, 99.
Lyons, 22, 54, 59, 118.

Machiavelli, 10, 11, 87.
Macon, 20.
Maestricht, 98.
Maine, 22.
Maistre, De, 75.
Margaret of Valois, 55, 89, 95, 96, 101.
Marillac, Archbishop, 9.
Marne, The, 117.
Marseilles, 50, 96, 113.
Mary of Guise, Regent of Scotland, 46, 55.
Mary Stuart, 7, 8, 55, 60, 95, 106.
Maximilian I., Emperor, 10.
Maximilian II., Emperor, 94, 103.
Mayenne, Duke of, 71-76, 79, 118, 123.
Meaux, 19, 22.
Melun, 117.
Mendoça, 49, 73.
Mercœur, Duke of, 55, 79, 80, 118.
Mercuriale, The, 5, 6.
Mesmes, Henri de, 93.
Metz, 46.
Michieli, 19, 49, 101.
Moncontour, Battle of, 27, 28, 32, 90.
Mons, 100.
Monsieur, Peace of, 36, 52, 109, 111.
Montauban, 16, 34.
Montereau, 117.
Montgomery, 19, 87.
Montluc, Bishop, 9, 110.
Montluc, Blaise de, 19, 21, 24, 25, 29, 51, 52, 93.
Montmorenci, Anne, Duke of and Constable, 7, 17, 28, 36, 37, 46, 48, 49, 99, 110.
Montmorenci, Francis, Duke of and Marshal, 36, 37.
Montmorenci, Henry (Damville), Duke of and Constable, 37-39, 41, 71, 114, 118.
Montmorenci, House of, 7-9, 13, 17, 30, 36, 45.
Montpellier, 16, 22.

Montpensier, Catherine, Duchess of, 41, 46, 55, 71-75.
Moutpensier, Charlotte of, Abbess of Jouarre, 106.
Montpensier, Duke of, 41, 55.
Moreo, 57.

Nantes, 19.
Nantes, Edict of, 22, 43, 44, 120.
Nassau, Louis of, 100, 101.
Navarre, 58. See Antony, Henry IV., Jeanne d'Albret.
Nemours, Duke of, 47, 75, 79, 118.
Nemours, Duchess of, 71.
Nérac, 21, 88.
Netherlands, The, 2, 3, 28, 38, 48, 54, 96-100, 104-110.
Nevers, Duchy of, 47.
Nîmes, 16, 22, 34, 37.
Normandy, 4, 12, 19-22, 26, 56, 59, 77, 80, 113, 114, 121.
Notre Dame de Clery, 26.

Orange, William of, 5, 6, 97-99, 104-109.
Orleans, 22, 23, 26, 49, 59, 67, 117.

Pacification, Edict of, 15.
Pamiers, Bishop of, 120.
Panigarola, Bishop of Asti, 62, 66, 76.
Paris, 22, 26, 28, 33, 45, 49-53, 57, 60, 63, 65, 67, 70-82, 88, 96, 101, 114-118.
Parliaments, 2, 4, 16, 24, 25, 64, 67, 92, 120, 122.
Parliament of Aix, 70.
Parliament of Dijon, 121.
Parliament of Nantes and Rennes, 70.
Parliament of Paris, 4, 15, 47, 49, 50, 69, 70, 74-76, 120.
Parliament of Rouen, 25, 70, 77.
Parliament of Toulouse, 20, 25, 70, 121.
Parma, Duke of, 74, 107, 109, 116.
Pasquier, E., 120.
Paul IV., Pope, 4.
Paulette, The, 121.
Pelletier, Curé, 75.
Penthièvre, House of, 55.
Peronne, 53.
Phillip II. of Spain, 10, 28, 57, 64, 73, 78, 95-97, 103, 106, 109.
Picardy, League of, 53-56, 58.
Plessis, Treaty of, 107.
Poissi, Colloquy of, 14-16.
Poitiers, 5.
Poitou, 19, 21, 37, 42.
Politiques, The, 36-38, 52, 59, 71, 74-76, 78, 82, 105, 114-116.
Pons, Marquis of, 58.
Porcian, Prince of, 19.
Portugal, King of, 96.
Portugal, Queen of, 95.
Pragmatic Sanction, 31, 122.
Priali, 33.
Provence, 20, 24, 59, 79, 113, 114, 118.
Pyrenees, The, 16, 20, 21, 58, 78.

Renée, Duchess of Ferrara, 45.
Rennes, 50, 70.

INDEX.

Requesens, 106.
Réveil Matin, The, 56.
Rheims, 67, 77.
Rhine, The, 39.
Rhone, The, 21.
Richelieu, 5, 44, 88.
Rochelle, 5, 20, 41, 42, 99, 104.
Rochelle, Treaty of, 36.
Rohan, Duke of, 19.
Rose, Bishop of Senlis, 62, 75, 76.
Rosières, 54, 55.
Rouen, 23, 70, 76, 116, 117.
Roye, Eléonore de, 7, 86.

St. André, Marshal, 49.
St. Bartholomew, Massacre of, 18, 28-33, 36, 41, 51-55, 60, 75, 82, 86, 89, 93, 101-106, 111.
St. Denis, Battle of, 28, 37, 94.
St. Germain, Assembly of, 92, 99.
St. Germain, Treaty of, 25, 29, 96.
St. Jean d'Angely, 28.
Saintonge, 113.
Salic Law, 41, 55, 63, 81.
Saluzzo, 79.
Sancerre, 104.
Saône, The, 21.
Saracini, 56.
Savoy, Duke of, 22, 78, 79, 118.
Schomberg, 27, 96.
Seine, The, 26, 89.
Sixteen, The, 66, 70, 72-76, 78.
Sixtus V., Pope, 65, 66, 116.
Smith, Sir T., 19.
Soissons, Count of, 41, 82.
Somme, The, 43, 117.
Soranzo, 5.
Sorbonne, The, 69, 76, 78, 122.
Strozzi, 47, 100.
Sulli, 12, 123.
Swiss, The, 24, 30, 60, 61, 80, 97.

Tanquerel, J., 64.
Tassis, 57.
Tavannes, Gaspard de Sauex, 19, 29, 32, 37, 45, 48, 49, 59, 76, 80-82, 87, 88, 90, 114, 118, 120, 124.

Tavannes, Marshal, 20, 21, 24, 26, 28, 53, 76, 93, 111, 112.
Teligni, 33, 99.
Tende, Comte de, 24.
Three Bishoprics, The, 38, 85, 118.
Tornabuoni, 11, 21.
Toulouse, 20, 24, 50, 59, 70, 71.
Tours, 43, 120.
Trent, Council of, 14, 57, 78.
Troyes, 20, 77.
Troyes, Bishop of, 13.
Troyes, Treaty of, 95.
Turenne, Vicomte de, 37, 44.
Tuscan Envoys, 5, 11, 13, 21, 50, 56, 60, 89, 90, 109, 115.
Tuscany, Duke of, 118.

University of Paris, 49, 50, 74.
University of Toulouse, 20.
Usez, Bishop of, 14.
Utrecht, Union of, 107.

Valence, Bishop of, 14.
Valenciennes, 3, 98, 100, 101.
Valois, House of, 17, 26, 48, 53, 55, 56, 60, 63, 69, 119.
Vassi, 16, 49.
Vaudois, The, 22.
Velai, The, 20, 22, 67, 71.
Vendôme, Cardinal, 82.
Vendôme, Duke of, 7.
Venetian Envoys, 5, 11, 13, 19, 28, 32, 40, 49, 69, 86-88, 101, 103.
Vielleville, Marshal, 5, 28, 93, 94.
Villars, Marshall, 118.
Villeroy, 123.
Vindiciæ contra tyrannos, The, 35.
Viscounts, The, 28.
Vivarais, The, 20, 22.

Walsingham, 98.

Ybarra, 73.

Zealand, 99, 100, 108.

www.ingramcontent.com/pod-product-compliance
Lightning Source LLC
Chambersburg PA
CBHW020101170426
43199CB00009B/364